Architectural Design

Architecture + Film II

Guest-edited by Bob Fear

W WILEY-ACADEMY

Architectural Design
Vol 70 No 1 January 2000

ISBN 0-471-62975-8
Profile No 143

Editorial Offices
International House
Ealing Broadway Centre
London W5 5DB
T: + 44 (0)20 8326 3800
F: + 44 (0)20 8326 3801
E: info@wiley.co.uk

Editor
Maggie Toy

Guest Editor
Bob Fear

Managing Editor
Helen Castle

Production
Mariangela Palazzi-Williams

Art Director
Christian Küsters

Design Assistant
Owen Peyton Jones

Advertisement Sales
01243 843272

Editorial Board
Denise Bratton
Peter Cook
Massimiliano Fuksas
Charles Jencks
Jan Kaplicky
Robert Maxwell
Jayne Merkel
Monica Pidgeon
Antoine Predock
Leon van Schaik

Photo Credits
ᴀᴅ Architectural Design
Credits for film stills pp 6–95 are
all provided inside the publication in
the captions adjacent to the images;
p 70 © Gerald Zugmann;
p 71 © Punctum/H-ch Schink;
p 73 © Richard Holttum;
p 78, 80 and 81 courtesy the press
office of the Tate Gallery, London
pp 86 and 93 © Jens Willebrand.

ᴀᴅ Plus
p 98+ portrait photo: Dan Cornish
p 99+ 3-D computer drawings of Telenor
Telecommunications Headquarters by
Joey Myers, Jonathan Ward, Jin Ah Park
and Joe Herrin at ɴʙʙᴊ
p 99+ model of Vulcan Northwest,
photo: Fred Housel;
p 101+ National Gallery of Berlin,
photos: Hendrich Blessing;
p101+ interior of Deloitte & Touche
Headquarters, photos: Chuck Choi,
Dan Cornish and Wayne Fujii;
p 101+ Seoul Dome model,
photo: John Lodge of ɴʙʙᴊ;
p 101+ 3-D interior perspective by
Jonathan Ward, Mike Amaya, Joey Myers
and Jonathan Emmet of ɴʙʙᴊ;
p 102+ colour perspective of
New York Police Academy:
Paul Davis of Ellerbe Beckett;
p 102+ model of New York Police Academy,
photo: Dan Cornish;
p 103+ New York Psychiatric Institute,
photos: Dan Cornish;

p 103+ State University of New York,
photo: Dan Cornish
p 103+ Kwun Tong Town Centre model,
photo: Maria Ryan Wagner;
pp 104+ and 105+ courtesy Jakob and
MacFarlane;
pp 106+ and 107+ all photos
© Michael Hintlian;
p 108+ portrait photos courtesy
StephensonBell;
p 109+ Quay Bar, courtesy StephensonBell,
photos: © David Grandorge;
p 109+ Manchester Convention Centre,
courtesy StephensonBell;
p 110+ Smithfield Buildings, courtesy
StephensonBell, © David Grandorge;
p 112+ photos courtesy Jeffrey James
Design.

Subscription Offices UK
John Wiley & Sons Ltd.
Journals Administration Department
1 Oldlands Way, Bognor Regis
West Sussex, PO22 9SA
T: +44 (0)1243 843272
F: +44 (0)1243 843232
E: cs-journals@wiley.co.uk

Subscription Offices USA and Canada
John Wiley & Sons Ltd.
Journals Administration Department
605 Third Avenue
New York, NY 10158
T: +1 212 850 6645
F: +1 212 850 6021
E: subinfo@wiley.com

Annual Subscription Rates 2000
Institutional Rate: UK £135
Student Rate: UK £60
OUTSIDE UK
Institutional Rate: US $225
Student Rate: US $105

ᴀᴅ is published six times a year.
Prices are for six issues and include
postage and handling charges.
Periodicals postage paid at Jamaica,
NY 11431. Air freight and mailing in the
USA by Publications Expediting Services
Inc, 200 Meacham Avenue, Long Island,
NY 11003

Single Issues UK: £19.99
Single Issues outside UK: US $32.50
Order two or more titles and postage
is free. For orders of one title ad
£2.00/US $5.00. To receive order
by air please add £5.50/US $10.00

Postmaster
Send address changes to ᴀᴅ c/o Expediting
Services Inc, 200 Meacham Avenue,
Long Island, NY 11003

Printed in Italy. All prices are subject
to change without notice.
[ISSN: 0003-8504]

Front cover
Smirnoff 'Smarienberg' commercial
Images courtesy Lowe Howard Spink
(Digital remix by Shazad Ahmed)

Architecture + Film II
Guest Editor Bob Fear

𝐀𝐃   Architectural Design +

Since 1930, *Architectural Design* has been constantly changing. It has moved through various sizes, layouts and incarnations – advertising supplement, monthly magazine – before ultimately arriving at the successful bimonthly publication it is today. On its 70th anniversary, it is then only fitting that we should ensure △'s place at the forefront of design and architectural thinking with a redesign of both the publication itself and the logo. Last year, we held an invited competition to find a new design concept for the publication. The most outstanding entry came from a young London-based designer, Christian Küsters who introduced a totally new look, an innovative typeface and a more flexible layout. There are, however, editorial as well as design changes. A new back section △+ has been developed by the Managing Editor Helen Castle to accommodate one-off articles as well as regular series, such as Practice Profile and Site Lines. These improvements complement the existing core of the publication, the themed issue. As before, we will be continuing to pursue subjects that challenge existing architectural preconceptions, engage with the latest design technologies and take on new frontiers. This is particularly noticeable in the next issue, *Space Architecture*, in which we will show the extraterrestrial environment to be the most fertile and open field for architectural exploration in the 21st century. Other forthcoming titles for 2000 are: *Contemporary Processes in Architecture*, *The Transformable House*, *Architecture of the Tragic* and *Architecture and Fashion*.

The glamour and idealism of the film world is irresistible. Even in its most gritty or lifelike projections, it has the ability to transcend the mundanities of real life. For architects, however, the fascination with film extends beyond the surface appeal of the celluloid image. There are tangible parallels and similarities in the design and production processes of architecture and film. Rem Koolhaas, who was a movie scriptwriter before becoming an architect, has said that there is little difference between the two activities. Patrick Keiller, who has taken the opposite direction professionally, training as an architect before becoming a film-maker, has explained (see interview on p 82) how he turned to film in an attempt to communicate architectural qualities in built structures.

It has become increasingly apparent since *Architectural Design's* highly successful 1994 issue on architecture and film just how wide and rich the seam is between the two media. Whereas the first edition discussed the relationship between film and architecture by studying the popular examples of *Blade Runner*, *The Hudsucker Proxy* and *The Fountainhead*, Bob Fear, the guest-editor of this issue has taken a multi-faceted approach. The publication is organised chronologically and takes in articles spanning the entire 20th century, including Soviet silent films, German Expressionists, cult films about sex in 60s London and LA disaster movies. Different genres are also explored – comedy, horror, disaster, cyborg … In the latter part of the publication, the relationship between architecture and film is further elaborated on: in 'Sideshow to Arthouse', Edwin Heathcote gives an account of the most concrete manifestation of the meeting of architecture and film, the cinema as building type. We are then taken behind the camera when two directors, Murray Grigor and Karl Sabbagh, give their accounts of making films about architecture; the former about an architect, Carlo Scarpa, and the latter about the construction of a building, the Tate Gallery at Bank. The circle is complete when Bob Fear ends the issue with a feature that looks at how architects have been directly inspired by the science-fiction aesthetics of James Bond movies. *Maggie Toy*

Liquid Architecture

Eisenstein and *Film Noir*

Peter Lyssiotis and Scott McQuire glue together a few fragments of a possible map for piecing together the city in film. They draw from the early pioneering visions of Sergei Eisenstein and Fritz Lang as well as the Chandleresque *'noir'* world of shadows and light as depicted in the 1998 *Dark City*.

The modern city is, in part, a celluloid invention. While the city inhabits the cinescape as a composite of film set, narrative setting and social consciousness, film has equally permeated architectural imagination across the century. Frequently, the city is not the explicit subject of a film; rather a backdrop, an envelope, an aura, perhaps evident only in a few fleeting scenes. How much of *Metropolis* (1926), for example, is actually devoted to the miniature cityscape painstakingly modelled for its production? Yet it is Lang's Manichean vision of life in the vertical city – inspired by his shipboard encounter with Manhattan – that is remembered, rather than the unconvincing narrative resolution of differences between capital and labour, head and heart.

How then, to map the city in film? Should one follow genres? Chronology? Or rather find moments that lurch out unexpectedly, revealing traces of the invisible city, which, as Alexander Kluge once said, is 'the urban structure ... lodged in our nerves, feelings, knowledges'. Here are a few fragments of a possible map, pieces that do not conform to a single grid or scale, the unedited shots of a lost film, which, in a soon-to-be-forgotten predigital age, lie awaiting an editor's glue.

Glass City

In 1926 Sergei Eisenstein travels to Berlin, where *Battleship Potemkin* (1925) is screened to great acclaim. Eisenstein and his cameraman Eduard Tisse stay at the Hotel Hessler, a striking example of the new glass and steel architecture. He jots down some notes for a film scenario, which will become known as the *Glass House* project. Around the same time, another Berlin resident, Walter Benjamin, influenced by Paul Scheerbart's 1913 monograph *Glasarchitektur*, is commencing his monumental *Passagenwerk*, which will occupy him for the rest of his life. In his 1929 essay on Surrealism, Benjamin will extol the 'revolutionary virtues' of living in a glass house. In June 1930, when Eisenstein is in Hollywood searching for a suitable subject for a film to be produced by Paramount Studios, his attention is caught by an article in the *New York Times Magazine* on Frank Lloyd Wright's project for a high-rise glass tower. Eisenstein writes a synopsis in English for *The Glass House*, which includes a prologue, 'Symphony of Glass', and five narrative parts that deal with the social life experienced in glass buildings. The drama revolves around the new conditions of transparency, and the fact that it is suddenly possible to see many things that were previously hidden. Part 1 is titled 'We do not see each other', because, as Eisenstein scrawls, the residents 'do not want to see each other'. In Part 2, a poet 'comes and opens our eyes'. In Part 3, the residents begin to notice each other, but 'the effect is the opposite – they put walls between each other'. The poet makes an impassioned speech that results in the formation of a *nudiste* association. Part 4 depicts a 'tailor' faction opposing the 'graduation in nudity' and 'competition becomes battle'. Part 5 details the rise of 'plots, plots, plots' and the eventual suicide of the poet. Eisenstein's notes conclude: 'Impossibility to continue like that smashing of the house.'

Paramount reject Eisenstein's scenario, but its concern with the new configurations of social existence and sexual desire produced by urban density and architectural transparency would recur periodically in cinema, most prominently in Hitchcock's *Rear Window* (1954), which relocates Eisenstein's collective drama onto the psychosocial plane of the individual viewer/ voyeur. In the 1990s *Sliver,* Phillip Noyce repeats a similar scenario with Sharon Stone as the unwitting subject of surveillance via secret cameras embedded in a smart apartment building. In the era of the high-security home, electronic windows never close.

Eisenstein's *Glass House* project is never made; instead he explores the Piranesian spaces of the medieval palace in *Ivan the Terrible* (1945).

Towards the end of his life, Eisenstein recalled his youth as a member of Agitprop in 1920 when he lived, along with many others, in a railway carriage in the Smolensk railyard. In the course of describing the vast

sidings with their labyrinthine tracks disappearing out of sight, and remembering the lonely experience of 'hours spent at night searching for your car along miles of silent railroad cars', he evokes the aerial view of 'the lights of Los Angeles, a city 40 miles long merging with the mist'. The horizontal celluloid city remains a far cry from his imagined city of glass in which transparency and illumination could still be a metaphor for the revolutionary transformation of consciousness.

In 1947, the year before he died, Eisenstein returns once again to the *Glass House* project, this time in connection with a 3-D (stereoscopic) film. The poet's suicide scene – first drafted only a year after Mayakovsky's suicide had signalled the crisis of the Soviet avantgarde and the rise of Stalinist terror – is mentioned as an example of stereoscopy used for shock effect.

citizens to perceive what is really happening. Perhaps these conspiracy theories are, in some measure, a response to a general loss of existential co-ordinates experienced in the metropolis. The modern city, filled with strangers, is the quintessential realm of random encounters; an intoxicating world of possibilities shadowed by the risk that a single step off the main street could plunge one into an abyss. The detective story maps this existential dilemma, stretched between the poles of identity and law. But how do you remain true to yourself when the whole environment is corrupt? This problem emerges with Chandler's Philip Marlowe. It seems no accident that he resides in Los Angeles, the world's first automotive city, and the global home of the movies.

Urban alienation is inevitably cloaked with sexuality. In *film noir* the city is often figured as a woman, seductive, sphinxlike and dangerous. A lonely man

The modern city has often been figured as a labyrinth with a criminal mastermind lying spiderlike and unseen at its centre

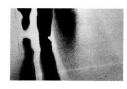

Paranoid City

In *Dark City* (1998) a man wakes up in a room with a dead woman who has been brutally murdered. His memory is hazy, fragmented. He can't remember what happened, or even his own name. The film conjures a compendium of *noir* elements: seedy hotels, shadowy streets, a string of dead women, hard-boiled cops, a hero accused of murder, a torch singer wife, all set in what seems to be the *noir* heyday of the 1940s. The plot, as with so many *noir* tales, revolves around a search for memory and identity. Beneath the surface of everyday life lurks a massive conspiracy. Someone – a group of strangers – is after him. They want to kill him, but no one believes it. The quest for personal identity becomes a journey into the underbelly of the city, an exposure of its double life.

The modern city has often been figured as a labyrinth with a criminal mastermind lying spiderlike and unseen at its centre. From Conan Doyle's Professor Moriarty to Souvestre's mysterious Fantomas and Lang's malignant Dr Mabuse, the power of the criminal genius to control apparently unconnected events is in inverse proportion to the capacity of ordinary

searches among the shifting crowds for a moral compass. Is redemption to be found in love? Or in death? Who will pay the price for his desire? If Chandler located Marlowe's moral struggle primarily at an individual level, this orientation was accentuated by the cinematic grafting of the Marlowe character to the Bogart persona. In narrative terms, *Dark City* keeps faith with the *noir* tradition in which redemption from the nightworld is the task of an isolated individual. But the film's visual design suggests another route. Its fable of strange beings who conjure a city out of nothing, and change it overnight to implement their own plans, not only exploits new cinematic possibilities of digital imaging, but offers a parable for the mutation of the cityscape that proceeded apace with urban 'redevelopments' in the 1980s and 1990s. Our cities dissolve and coagulate around us, populations are dispersed, lives rerouted, identities changed, subject to invisible forces that render the metropolis as liquid as the movies that once claimed to be its mirror. Conspiracy theories circling around an evil genius, like dark fairy tales that always blame the (bad) woman, are one way of putting a face to an implacable economic system. But these fables risk transforming urban politics into nostalgia. We should also remember that Marlowe's sunshine and *noir* California was the birthplace of post-Reaganite *laissez-faire* global capitalism. ᴐ

All images
Original photography
by Peter Lyssiotis

Vsevolod Pudovkin
and the Theory of Montage

Through the work of Vsevolod Pudovkin, Heather Puttock explores how montage film-making in Soviet silent films employed an architectonic model that utilised separate, seemingly unrelated, film strips as building blocks. It was through the dynamic editing of these films – a Marxist dialectical process of antithesis, synthesis and thesis – that the full revolutionary effect of the genre was intended to impact on the spectator.

The cinema of montage – a cinema in which specific meanings are produced through a foregrounded, often startling, juxtaposition of shots – is synonymous with Soviet cinema of the 1920s. The reasons for its existence can also be linked to the dominant ideology in the Soviet Union at that time. A commitment to the reality of the Revolution, and a vision of a developed Socialist state, galvanised many Soviet film-makers to foster a theory of editing that appeared to them axiomatic: montage was a process that operated to Marxist dialectics.[1] Yet the principles underpinning montage did not lend themselves exclusively to dialectics. The process was a fusion of many different movements, none of them inherently Marxist. Indeed, montage can be located within a nexus of Modernist ideas that started life in the pre-Revolution avantgarde, and which affected art and architecture long before they had any influence on film.

In post-Revolution Russia, film-makers were radically deconstructing film, literally stripping the moving picture back to its raw celluloid to analyse the theoretical and dramatic qualities of purposive juxtaposition. They saw how relationships between shots could be governed by compositional or graphic elements, by rhythm and movement within shots and by the tone of the shot content itself. And so when, in 1925, the Politbüro endorsed a state ruling not to intervene in matters of style and form in the arts, Soviet cinema was ready to enter its most passionate and formally challenging period. The film-makers may have been pragmatic in correlating montage and Marxism, but their inchoate findings soon became a credo. Montage's most compelling rhetorician was Sergei Eisenstein. He welded his theories to the Revolution, and his films have come to work metonymically for that period.[2] For film-maker and theorist Vsevolod Pudovkin, the key process of montage was in linkage. He adopted an architectonic model for film, arguing that the separate strips of film were building blocks that, when arranged in a series, could expand and build upon an idea.[3]

that found in its relationship to other pieces of film. Film art began when the director combined various pieces of film that stimulated different reactions in the spectator.[6] Kuleshov's other legacy lies in his negotiation of the problem of the cinema actor and the need to establish the specificity of film over theatre. In his concept of the *naturschik*, or model actor, Kuleshov replaced the psychological embodiment of character with the physical exteriorisation of intention, maintaining that for every human emotion there was a corresponding external movement. But it was a delight in the mechanics of industry that formed the greatest

Montage sought to resolve the raw material into its constituent elements long before the film was assembled

The Revolution and a new emphasis on art as a social product geared towards the needs of the proletariat gave Modernist ideas an unprecedented social and political role in the Soviet Union. The Futurists, with their rejection of traditional aesthetic values, were perfectly poised to respond to Lenin's call for the creative intelligentsia to produce a new art for agitational purposes. Cubo-Futurist poet Vladimir Mayakovsky did not believe language was an inviolate system of communication, and in his poetry he intruded upon the traditionally untouchable fundaments of syntax and word. His creativity with language convinced many artists that if poetry and literature could withstand such a transfiguration, then other forms of art with their own idioms could also achieve a similar process of transformation.[4]

The idea that art is a language is the basis on which Pudovkin's colleague and mentor, Lev Kuleshov, predicated his work. After the civil war, the Soviet Union had an extremely limited supply of raw film stock. One way for the cinema to develop was through the re-editing of old films. Kuleshov formed his own workshop where he and his colleagues would 'arrest' old film negatives from the studios and re-edit the 'rubbish filmed by the bourgeoisie' in order to turn it into revolutionary art. This phenomenon of creation through destruction can also be found in Cubo-Futurist architecture, where the desire for a new form of expression manifested itself in the maximum transformation of the bourgeois urban scene.[5] The artistic legacy that Kuleshov bequeathed to Pudovkin and Eisenstein was the discovery that inherent in a single piece of edited film were two strengths: its own and

influence on Kuleshov's theories. In American cinema, Kuleshov saw not actors, but the organs of the definitive mechanisation of life. The physiology of the working man was, as Kuleshov perceived it, Constructivism based on machine art.[7]

Constructivism arose from the struggle to establish new forms of art, to effect the aspirations of the revolutionary proletariat and enhance the intellectual existence of society as a whole – hence the movement's easy acquiescence to machine production and the media of mass communication. Early Constructivists had seen this taking effect through the construction of the environment, not through its depiction, and this accorded with the theories of Production Art,[8] which suggested that the purpose of the artist was to create an objective reality from the things composing the environment. To achieve this, the theorists behind Production Art advocated a stringent utilitarian approach that accentuated ideological content through the subjugation of artistic formulation.[9] This culture of things, or *Veschizm*, developed into a labour construction of art. The nature of artistic activity was replaced by producing, and with it came a change in semantics: art equalled labour.[10] Film, with its technical base, its industrialised mode of production and process of assembly represented the apotheosis of art as production and artist (the director) as engineer. In his theories and work, Pudovkin maintained that editing was the 'foundation of film art'. It was not something, however, that simply occurred in the cutting room. Montage was a meticulous construction of interdependent pre-planning that sought to resolve the raw material into its constituent elements long before the film was assembled.[11]

A recurrent theme in Pudovkin's work is the politically naive character who comes to political consciousness and militancy when faced with the consequences of her/his political inaction. In *Mother* (1926), set during the 1905 Revolution, a woman innocently betrays her revolutionary son to the authorities. After he is imprisoned she continues to meet his compatriots and gradually becomes involved in their activities. She smuggles a note to her son in prison, outlining an escape planned to coincide with the May Day demonstrations. The son escapes but is shot during the demonstration. His mother picks up the red banner and leads the procession. In *The End of St Petersburg* (1927) the theme is the same: a starving peasant goes to St Petersburg in search of food. He gets a job at a factory but there, an agitation is in progress. Ignorant of what is going on, the peasant becomes a blackleg. When he realises the political significance of the situation he rampages through the factory offices and is jailed. The First World War is declared and the jails are emptied to conscript troops. The peasant is sent to the trenches and the factory starts to produce munitions. The peasant persuades his battalion to defect and leads its return, as an aspiring Red Army, to St Petersburg where it storms the Winter Palace and overthrows the provisional government.

Pudovkin maintained that the audience would only recognise a theme when the director had found a specific phenomenon to depict it. Each relevant aspect of this was to be contained in a single shot and only when the single shots were linked together would they depict the total phenomenon. If the montage process had been properly planned, the edited shots would form a new relationship that would reveal the theme.[12] This idea of linkage contrasts with the collision of frames that Eisenstein proposed for the purposes of making direct intellectual statements and abstract ideas. Pudovkin rarely engaged in intellectual abstraction, believing that associational montage would expunge the aesthetically valid figurative expression. But that is not to say that the spectator was not the perceptual target. Pudovkin believed that editing was the 'compulsory and deliberate guidance of the thoughts and associations of the spectator'.[13] Yet, the emotional excitement that he wished to evoke in the spectator did not require him to go outside the film's diegesis, even when the montage was at its most symbolic. In *Mother*, for example, the sequence in which the son plans his escape from the prison is intercut with ice breaking up and floating down the river. These scenes are then intercut with the marchers and soldiers moving towards the

factory where the demonstration will take place. As the river becomes more clogged with ice the number of troops increases. But the metaphor does have a narrative function because the river passes by the prison and provides the medium by which Pavel, the son, escapes and joins the demonstration. Similarly, in *The End of St Petersburg*, a series of energetic montage sequences contrast corpulent businessmen speculating on munitions stocks with soldiers dying in muddy trenches. The cognitive association is the correlation between human misery and capitalism, but there is also a narrative function in that the peasant

<hr>

The construction, the layering of extraneous material, builds up the dramatic situation, and Pudovkin believed, ensured that the captivated spectator received the most forceful of revolutionary impulses

used to work for the factory. This construction, the layering of extraneous material, builds up the dramatic situation and, Pudovkin believed, ensured that the captivated spectator received the most forceful of revolutionary impulses.[14]

A second aspect of ensuring the requisite response in the audience was Pudovkin's decision to cast actors whose physicality represented the desired expression of the film. Actors, like the selected phenomena, were raw material for the director to construct, and Pudovkin believed that the actor should not affect the spectator by psychological means, but that the director should indicate emotion through images saturated with plastic, or externally expressive, ideas.[15] In *Mother*, for example, where Pavel receives a note saying he will be set free, Pudovkin does not show his face lighting up with joy. Instead, he focuses on the nervous play of his hands, intercut with shots of a swollen river, sunlight playing on water, birds splashing in a pond and finally a child laughing.

The transformation of the actor's function represents the pinnacle of montage, for it shows how the process had transformed human nature and created a new socialist being. In its myriad of diverse influences, the underlying objective of montage was the same: to create a new material environment and effect a new way of thinking. But it was not simply through the application of dialetics that this was achieved. Instead, it was in a form of Constructivism, as exemplified by Pudovkin's architectonic model of film making, that montage found its most cogent expression. ⌂

Footnotes
1. *Film Form*, 'A Dialectical Approach to Film Form', Sergei M Eisenstein, Harcourt Brace (New York), 1949, pp 22–44.
2. Scenes of the proletariat storming the Winter Palace in Eisenstein's *October* (1927), are often erroneously used as documentary footage in representations of the Revolution.
3. *Film Technique and Film Acting*, VI Pudovkin, translated and edited by Ivor Montagu, Vision Press Ltd and The Mayflower Publishing Company Limited (London), 2nd edition, 1958, p 24.
4. *Soviet Architecture: The Search for New Solutions in the 1920s and 1930s*, Selim O Khan-Magomedov, Thames and Hudson Ltd. (London), 1987, p 62.
5. Ibid, p 75.
6. *Kino: A History of the Russian and Soviet Film*, Jay Leyda, George Allen & Unwin, London, 1960, p 175.
7. *Inside the Film Factory New Approaches to Russian and Soviet Cinema*, 'Kuleshov's experiments and the new anthropology of the actor', Mikhail Yampolsky. Richard Taylor and Ian Christie (eds.), Routledge, London, 1991, p 49.
8. *Soviet Architecture*, Khan-Magomedov, p 146.
9. Ibid, p 146.
10. Ibid, p 147.
11. *Film Technique and Film Acting*, Pudovkin, pp 26–55.
12. Ibid, pp 26–55.
13. Ibid, p 73.
14. Ibid, p 52.
15. Ibid, p 135.

Spaces of the Psyche
in German Expressionist Film

The emotional intensity of film space was at its height in
the German Expressionist period, when film-makers sought
to express the inner angst of the characters through
their Gothic labyrinthine settings. Hans Dieter Schaal
here traces the way in which the Expressionist impulse
transferred itself from the canvas on to the big screen in
1920s Germany, resulting in some of the most dramatic
works of film architecture, ranging from the nightmarish
fairground backdrops of *The Cabinet of Dr Caligari* to the
shadowy streets of Fritz Lang's *M*.

Film architecture – interiors and exteriors –
is always architecture that has been depicted,
photographed, turned into an image. It embraces
the actors and scenes like an air space that has
become visible, like a built coat, a petrified robe,
a stage set. Its presence defines the setting, the
social position of the characters and their inner
moods. The openings in the walls and ceilings,
the windows, doors and slits, determine the
geometry of incidental light. Visible light sources
complete the picture. Film architecture is
fictional architecture. It is unimportant whether
a city, a building, a room exists in reality or
whether only the facades have been built up.
Film architecture is an architecture of meaning.
There is nothing in the frame that is not
important and does not have something to say.
Of course, this architecture is constructed, and
its importance appreciated only for the short
moment of being filmed; after that it rots away
as a tiresome ruin or is taken down, unless it
becomes part of a studio tour. It lives its
essential life in the film, as a new, atmospheric
truth. Camera and film have transformed it from
studio reality to media fiction. Film architecture
works in statements and images, with built
psychology, spiritual spaces, spiritual
landscapes. Film space is an emotional place
made up of walls, light and shade. The more
intense, brilliant or melancholic the atmosphere
becomes, the more powerful its effect in film.
This unity of mood between character and
place has been sought from the very beginning.
German Expressionist films were the great
pioneers here – even if on a somewhat
exaggerated plane – making a worldwide impact.
The heroes of these films, threatened by both
inside and outside forces, often mad and
communicating by means of supernatural
powers, roam with the exalted gestures of
silent film through a labyrinth of narrow alleys
that can represent both a medieval city and
a spiritual space that has become visible.

The Expressionists fought against impressionistic
superficiality; they no longer wanted merely to show
illuminated external worlds, but agitated inner worlds.
The Scream by Edvard Munch (1895) tells the story of
the human face, with wide-open eyes and mouth; the
cry remains silent, the eyes are staring at the new
century with anguish and horror – developing cities,
exploding world wars, new technologies with their
innovations and strange machinery. There is no chance
of escape from the relentless gears of time.

The Expressionists felt pressed into narrowness and
protested loudly. They revealed their internal traumas
and bloody wounds. They worked nervously and quickly
as if gripped by a fever. Sharp points, spikes, hectic
curves, signs like formulas, archaic masks, crazy
diagrams worthy of seismographic earthquake read-
outs, everything whirled around and fell like sediment
on to the screens. What Expressionist paintings had
formulated was realised as moving film image in
pictures such as *The Cabinet of Dr Caligari* (1919/20).
The melodramatic effect of an oil painting hanging in
a museum was far exceeded in the cinema's black box.
City, house, room, chamber, street, alley – every motif
is demonised and related directly to the characters as
a psychological element. These characters were seized
by panic as buildings crashed down on them; deaths
took place on steps and in alleyways. The built labyrinth
wrapped itself round their necks and choked them.

Two motives of the Expressionist film-maker became
apparent in the genre's storytelling. One was to portray
women as creatures who seduce men and destroy them
with anarchic sexuality: Asta Nielsen in *Girls Without
Homeland*, Fern Andra in *Genuine*, Louise Brooks in
Pandora's Box, Betty Amann in *Asphalt* and Marlene
Dietrich in *The Blue Angel*. The other motive was to
portray men driven to delusion by their own impulses,
resulting in neuroticism and madness: *The Cabinet of
Dr Caligari*, *The Golem*, *Nosferatu*, *Dr Mabuse* and *M*.

Opposite and above
The Cabinet of Dr Caligari
(Transit Films/BFI Stills)

13

The Expressionistic film searches for reality behind superficiality

The Expressionistic film searches for reality behind superficiality; it dwells on being in love with madness, with extremes, and on being out of balance. Therefore, it was perhaps inevitable that the major film of this genre – *The Cabinet of Dr Caligari* – took place in a mental asylum. The town that surrounds the asylum, as well as the fairground outside the town, are no different in their architectural language from the interiors of the asylum. Originally, Fritz Lang was to have been director with Alfred Kubin designing. However, three painters – Walter Reimann, Walter Röhrig and Hermann Warm – who belonged to the Storm, the Berlin group of Expressionists, ended up designing and constructing the *Caligari* world. Whilst it was unusual for established artists to paint two-dimensional film scenery, their innovative contribution temporarily helped rebuild the bridge between theatre and film.

When one views the film today, one is somehow irritated by the radical artwork; perhaps it detracts from the straightforward storytelling method to which we have become accustomed. It is the nonrealism that irritates: the exaggerated style, the Surrealism that wavers between African village huts and kindergarten parties, smoke-filled bars, and Stone Age cave drawings. But we are still fascinated by the stark, striking artificiality of this world. We are transported directly into the soul of Expressionistic painting. But the aesthetics are also associated with comic books, Punch and Judy shows and Christmas fairytales.

The architecture of *Caligari* consists of narrow, high rooms and lanes, inside and out. Everything is oblique and inclined. The walls are covered with strange signs and acute-angled figures. A winding, lopsided tropical green house becomes hostile, filled with carnivorous plants, huge leaves and climbing creepers. The labyrinth is completely enclosed and seemingly inescapable. Windows are no longer windows and trees are no longer trees. This architecture holds its occupants tight within its grasp, the walls built to fulfil this command. There is no chance of escape.

Through the illusionary composition of this film the viewer also becomes trapped in a subterranean 'inner-soul bubble', looking directly into the mouth of madness, denied a view of the real world, of real houses and real cities. Kafka's 'other side' is not far away. This world is the one behind the mirror, the imagined realm of dreams. Scenes begin and end with a slow, visible opening and closing of the camera shutter like eyelids.

This film also reflects the period of paranoia in prewar Germany; the threat of an all-consuming madness and our easy subservience to it. At the end of the film, all the town's people fill the asylum's atrium; a woman plays an invisible piano, Cesare embraces a flower. All gaze into emptiness, whilst speared on the points and spikes of the architecture. It's as if nobody wants to wake up from the dream; an elaborate warning against an increasingly real threat.

After the international success of *Caligari*, Wiene produced a second film, *Genuine*, in the same Expressionistic manner. Unfortunately, the crowds did not come twice, and *Caligari* remains the most well-known and successful Expressionist film. In *Genuine*, Fern Andra portrays the first female vampire in film history. Her character's film environment is not just painted backdrops, but a three-dimensionally constructed set with Expressionistically exaggerated features.

The bloodsucking Genuine lives in an opulent castle; a rounded, curved, erotic trap for her greedy victims.

Above
Genuine
(Transit Films/BFI Stills)

Opposite
M (BFI Stills)

The popular story, portrayed through *Salome* and *Electra* in literature and opera and which has its bloody culmination in *Lulu* and *Turandot*, is present here – the vamp who is nourished by men's blood. The film's architecture directly reflects *Genuine's* character and intentions. The Kafkaesque labyrinths of *Caligari* have given way to a sexually loaded, feminine environment. Some painted points and spikes remain, but found amongst them is a soft bed. The female vampire lies in wait as if she is a spider at the centre of a web. Fern Andra's trailing hair has the effect of an erotic promise, inviting wild, sexual thoughts. The architecture of her domain has only one goal – lethal seduction. The prominent architectural features of gates, doors, corridors and soft caves clearly represent the female body from which, once entered, there is no chance of escape. This preys on man's fear of woman's powerful, erotic, engulfing force. This film, along with *Caligari*, follows the mechanics of dreams. *Genuine* is a fantasy located in the imagination of overheated sexuality.

Translated from German
by Mel Court-Smith

The main character in Fritz Lang's *M*, the schizophrenic child-murderer played by Peter Lorre, provides the eyes through which we see the distorted, squalid streets of Berlin. The city is a system of dark lanes, shadowy streets, imposing walls, dingy rooms and confined spaces. Here, as in *Caligari*, is the strictly closed system that is controlled by underground criminals, suggesting deep-seated corruption. The mob, the police and frenzied citizens combine to track down the murderer. Again, we see a community threatened by madness, unable to trap and control it. The dark city is a unified machine, closing in on Lorre's character as he is hunted down like a deadly virus that infects the streets and threatens the 'natural' balance of the environment. No pity is offered for his madness; he himself is a victim of his own compulsiveness: 'Somebody is hunting me, it's myself. I have to run, run ... a voice inside is stalking me'. The Expressionistic view of the city directly reflects the interior of his mind.

Through these films, people first saw their own nightmares in the projected image. The film – and thus its architecture – had arrived at the core of its own effectiveness: a daydream space had become image with all the magic of an archetypal spell, a sober intoxication, a fictitious journey through world, life and ego. It was a journey through time and space, with picture stories of childhood, feelings, despair, love and hate, adventure, danger and death. Death witnessed in the cinema gives the viewer a sense of immortality, able to step out into the night as a survivor.

We see a community threatened by madness, unable to trap and control it

Subsequent film spaces and film architecture developed from the Expressionist space-cell with its atmosphere of exaggerated performances, fearful social mood, dramatic architecture and light, fused into one pictorial unity. Every great film director has tried to create this unity. Often, the chosen space, the building or city, becomes the leading character in the film: *Metropolis*, *Key Largo*, *Sunset Boulevard*, *The Silence*, *Viridiana*, *Manhattan*, *Roma*, *Subway*, *Batman*, *Psycho*, *Rear Window*, *Rebecca*, *The Blue Angel*, *The Last Laugh*, *Blade Runner*, *Pulp Fiction*. Films set in front of an empty white wall are scarcely conceivable. Space and architecture always need to be firmly established within the landscape, the city and the real or fictitious society. The place in which the story is set is crucial: on a skyscraper, in a village cottage, a castle, a palace at the bottom of the sea or in outer space. ⌀

Realising the
Spiritual City

Hans Poelzig and *The Golem*

In the Germany of 1920, Hans Poelzig famously designed and constructed a complete town consisting of 54 three-dimensional buildings for the film *The Golem*. Claudia Dillmann discusses the influences and means by which Poelzig realised his ambitious, Expressionistic designs, in which his spiritual convictions overcame the restraints of a depressed social climate and articulated a commentary on the struggles of a community in crisis, as well as on existing architectural traditions.

Hans Poelzig (1869–1936) was one of the few practising architects who have worked for the movies. Like Fritz Schumacher and Heinrich Tessenow, he belonged to the generation of designers whose work was situated somewhere between the traditional and Modernist movements. He created one of the greatest and architecturally rich film sets in cinematic history with his first movie *The Golem* (1920). The film's harmonic synthesis of buildings and figures, form and content is still convincing today.

Poelzig's work addressed both public and personal issues in the period just after Germany had lost the First World War. Considered avant-garde, he was fascinated by Gothic style and the cathedral as its central *Gesamtkunstwerk*. He was involved in the left-wing Council for the Arts and was interested in occultism, understanding architecture as a mystical art. His sketches for *The Golem* provide an insight into his working methods and the world of his imagination, which – when looking at their content and articulation – could be described as Expressionist.

The winter of 1918/19, and thus the end of the war, heralded a decisive event in Poelzig's life. While he was still Chief Architect for the city of Dresden, where there was no building work due to dire economic circumstances, he took on a commission from the prolific theatre director Max Reinhardt to convert a circus arena into a theatre holding 5,000 people. This included a gigantic dome Poelzig transformed into an enormous cave of stalactites using plaster cones.

Poelzig's thesis saw architecture as a means to heighten people's awareness; his aim was to create fantastic spaces, derived uncensored from his imagination. Ideas for a *Gesamtkunstwerk*, which bordered between the sacred and the profane, preoccupied him, along with his sketches for the unbuilt Salzburg Festival theatre. Since there was no public money for building, there were no commissions, and Poelzig was not alone in dreaming up ideas of boundless imagination. Bruno Taut and the members of the Glass Chain were also lost in reverie, designing glass palaces situated on Alpine peaks. Wenzel Hablik created the vision of a dissolving cathedral for an unrealised film project.

The first years after the war saw little building activity. Poelzig was head of a studio at the Prussian Academy of Arts and eventually established himself as a teacher at the Technical University in Berlin-Charlottenburg.

At this time, the generation of Modernists who had been born around 1900 would take on the smallest commission, even for a private house, and soon dominated the building market.

The possibility of successfully implementing his imaginative ideas was probably not the sole reason why Poelzig became involved in the movies. Another motivation might have been his friendship with the director, author and actor Paul Wegener (1874–1948), who had become famous with the film *The Student of Prague* (1913) and had since established himself with genre-bridging horror-romance fantasies. Wegener's affinity for this kind of material, his interest in Far Eastern esoterics and his concern with art theory and architecture also fuelled their friendship. In Paul Davidson, who at the time was the Director of the newly founded production company Ufa, Wegener had found a patron who would not only give him a free hand, but would also provide the means to realise a project like *The Golem* in the spring and summer of 1920.

The project was conceived by Ufa as a major film for which a large budget would be made available. As opposed to the set for another prestigious enterprise, Lubitsch's *Anna Boleyn* – for which a two-dimensional medieval London was built in the Ufa open-air studio with painted and staggered plywood walls – Poelzig designed a winding three-dimensional city with 54 buildings including a high ghetto wall. As his sketches reveal, the design was based on the consistent, rhythmic use of the Gothic pointed arch as the basic form, which represented the outline of the human body. This is omnipresent in the movie in the shape of the houses, the doors and gates, windows and interior spaces to which the actors willingly adapt. The materials used refer directly to the content of the story: like the golem, made from clay, the whole set is covered with a layer of plaster and straw to portray a town of half-timbered clay houses.

However, Poelzig did not intend to create 'real houses'. His sketches twist and turn exterior and interior spaces and buildings. In the movie, every building, especially the ghetto's gate, is given a specific, characteristic appearance; a 'face'. These buildings, in the spirit of Expressionism, represented a new approach. In *The Cabinet of Dr Caligari* (1919) the twists and turns of the set had been reduced to theatrical, two-dimensional, painted scenery. In *The Golem* the Expressionist filmic design was utilising three-dimensional shapes and spaces for the first time. The architecture of Golem city was considered by architecture critics to be so important that the film became the subject of analysis whilst still in production.

In both the analyses and the national and international reviews that were to follow, the term *gotisch* was being used almost unanimously. But while in German *gotisch* is merely used as a term describing the style, the

English Gothic has much broader connotations originating in 'black' romanticism. The connotations of the English term are closer to Poelzig's aims and the way in which he articulated his buildings. For Poelzig and a number of other artists, following the ideas of the art historian Wilhelm Worringer, *gotisch* meant 'vertical in character, odd, wrinkly, suffering, moved, exaggerated, fearsome, profound'. Opposed to this kind of Gothic is the Renaissance dictum: 'horizontal in character, light, straight, passive, calm, in harmony with the world, merry.' In the movie and in Poelzig's sketches these characteristics are realised in the central spaces featured in the story, namely, the ghetto and the castle. In the spirit of this idea of Gothic, Paul Wegener and Henrik Galeen, who was also fascinated by occultism, wrote the film's script.

The story is concerned with the attempted expulsion of the Jews from the Prague ghetto by the Habsburg Emperor Rudolf II. In order to prevent him, the Rabbi Loew creates a clay figure, the golem. With a necromantic spell Loew conjures the spirit of Ashtaroth and incarnates it within the golem. He does this

an angry, powerful force, which collapses the palace roof. In the following chaos the golem, ordered by Loew, saves the Emperor by catching a falling joist. The grateful Emperor withdraws his edict.

Back in the ghetto, Loew takes the life-giving *schem* away from the golem, despite resistance. As the community gathers in the synagogue for prayers of thanks, Loew discovers the forbidden lovers. He reactivates the golem with the *shem* and orders it to throw Florian from the tower. The golem resists subsequent attempts to take the *schem* away. In the struggle, the tower catches fire and collapses. The fire spreads to the ghetto. Loew manages to stop it with his magical powers. In the end, the golem breaks open the ghetto gate, but a small Christian girl whom it carries on its arm playfully grabs the *schem* and the golem dies. In a celebratory procession the Jews carry the dead colossus back to the ghetto.

The architecture of the set eloquently expresses the tone of the story as well as providing a commentary. The strong visual power that dominates nearly every shot allows the architecture to play a dramatic, multilayered role. In accordance with the principles of the Expressionist interpretation of Gothic, the centrally featured spaces are opposed to one another, thus symbolising a dualism. The question as to whether

In accordance with the principles of the expressionist interpretation of Gothic, the centrally featured spaces are opposed to one another thus symbolising a dualism

by placing the written word of the vital spell in an amulet (the *schem*) always to be worn on the golem's chest. Loew not only wants to demonstrate his magical abilities (and therefore his power) to the Emperor, he also wishes the golem to protect his daughter Miriam, of whose love for Florian, the messenger who handed the Emperor's edict to the Jews, he disapproves. At the Emperor's festival of roses, Loew, in the company of the golem, conjures up a vision of the Jews in the desert. Meanwhile, Miriam and Florian spend the night together in the ghetto. Loew's vision fails to make an impression on the Emperor, who – together with his court – mocks his powers. As a result, the vision itself develops

to interpret this as a complementary, causal principle or as an antithetical, inherently self-opposing structure is difficult to answer. Certain architectural elements, like the pointed arch of the door to the palace's throne room, are referential to both worlds. Some exaggerated ornamental elements present in the palace, characterising the court as decadent and superficial, also recur in the rabbi's house in a contorted fashion. In both locations, an important architectural element the throne room and the dwelling tower – is destroyed. The power of magic temporarily reinstates peace between both worlds, ensuring that they can live side by side. Magic unveils its threefold power: destructive (in the palace), redemptive (stopping the ghetto fire) and ambivalent (represented in the figure of the golem).

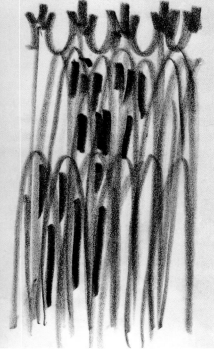

(combined in the gate tower) – communicate the image of the organic wholesomeness of an authentic society. The design of the filmic space tells the tale of the magic borderline between inorganic and organic elements, epitomised in the figure of the golem. At this self-referential point, *The Golem* becomes a film about the magic practice of the architect, since Poelzig himself attributed to architecture magical effects.

In a social climate that was determined by misery, mass unemployment, civil-war-like tensions and uncertainty following the collapse of the German Empire, Poelzig, with this film, succeeded in epitomising a generation of architects who had no commissions and swung between tradition and Modernism. Simultaneously, Poelzig and Wegener express their deep sympathy for a community's idealistic efforts to maintain its identity and authenticity amidst the struggles of society as a whole – through its spirituality, timeless awareness of its roots and resulting affirmation of its superior strength. In *The Golem* it was God's chosen people, in the artist's life, it was the hermetical sect.

After *The Golem*, Poelzig worked only twice again for the cinema. In 1923-24 he worked for Wegener's own production company on *Living Buddhas*, which proved to be a disastrous enterprise at a time of high inflation. The film, about the adventures of a group of Europeans involved with a Tibetan sect, disappeared unnoticed from the cinemas and has been missing ever since. Poelzig's few remaining sketches for this movie, showing the architectural blueprints for a temple and a cave for human sacrifice, are kept with the rest of his filmic work at the German Film Museum in Frankfurt, where they continue to be a popular subject for study. Due to the lack of funding, the set was made from papier-mâché, and the surviving photographs give an idea of how inadequate it must have seemed.

Poelzig was also involved in the design stage of Arthur von Gerlach's *Zur Chronik von Grieshuus* in 1923/24. An amorphous, half-derelict castle set in a dark and windy heathland, surrendering to the power of nature reconquering its territory, clearly carries Poelzig's signature. But, unlike on *The Golem*, Poelzig was allegedly not involved in the execution of the set. Squabbles within Ufa and competition from two star film architects Robert Herlth and Walter Röhrig might have lessened his interest in further film work. However, as an architect, he remained true to the medium of film in the following years. He designed extravagant cinemas for Berlin, one of which, the Capitol (1925), with its extraordinary spiral staircase, makes an elegant reference to *The Golem*. ಬಿ

Apart from its function within this dualism, the ghetto, as a (literally) closed architectural system, needs to be observed more closely. In a sociological sense, it symbolises the successful struggle of a community against the ruling class or society. With the design of the cavelike interior spaces and the pointed, compressed houses, Poelzig manages to express the confinement of the ghetto and the omnipresent pressures on the Jewish community. All the deformations, the dynamic application of fins and pillars and the spiral arrangement of stairs and towers, physically express the fear and unrest in the ghetto, which reaches its climax with the panic of the masses during the fire. But the ghetto is also full of spirituality, and the spiral staircase in the Rabbi's laboratory opens up like an ear towards the sky, allowing Loew to read the stars when standing on top of his tower.

Radically, Poelzig implemented ideas of an 'organic harmony' here which determined the architectural and artistic debate of the time. The derivation of architectural forms – from the outline of the human figure (the ducking houses, communicating with each other), from limbs (the sheltering and simultaneously confining 'arm' of the ghetto wall), from inner organs (the accentuated ribs in the cavelike interior spaces), from male (tower) and female (the wide gate) principles

Translated from German by Torsten Schmiedeknecht.

Modernism as Enemy

Film and the Portrayal of Modern Architecture

Here, Edwin Heathcote identifies an entire cinematic tradition in which Modernist buildings become the malevolent protagonist, whether the antiseptic Modernist villa encountered by Jacques Tati's bumbling Monsieur Hulot in *Mon Oncle*, or the bleak, soulless housing project in which the protagonists of Vittorio de Sica's *Bicycle Thieves* search for their stolen property.

Above and opposite
L'Avventura (BFI Stills)

Most criticism of architecture in films has concentrated on the visionary. From *Metropolis* to *Blade Runner* it is the vision of a future, whether bleak or optimistic, that has been of most interest to critics. In these films, directors have the chance to achieve whole new worlds, or at least cities, in a way that most architects can only dream of. There is, however, another strand of film architecture that acts not merely as a dramatic backdrop but virtually as a member of the cast. Architecture in film can undergo a transformation from static set to anthropomorphic participant in the lives of the characters. The character taken on by buildings is often malevolent and the chances of this happening seem to increase dramatically if the architecture is recognisably Modernist or futuristic. It is this transformation of modern architecture from mere film set to active enemy that I would like to briefly explore.

If we think of the symbolic significance of a door, we realise that it represents the threshold, the entrance to another realm; whether that realm is sacred or profane, public or private, the door is the guardian. It is one of the most powerful of architectural symbols;

if the anthropomorphic house has a mouth, then it is the door. Let us now think of Laurel and Hardy trying to get through a door. In *Going Bye-Bye* (1934), the hapless pair get stuck at the first stage. After Laurel's unsuccessful attempt to push the bell, Hardy tries and gets his finger stuck. An electric shock ensues as he is extricated and, as Laurel continues to investigate the button, the bell explodes and falls on Hardy's head. This is a door through which Laurel and Hardy are not welcome. Its is, of course, only one of man's such instances; doors do not like Laurel and Hardy. They slam shut, stranding them outside, they collapse, they are walked into. They are the ultimate illustration of the symbolic role of door as guardian (or nightclub bouncer). The reason that doors do not willingly admit them is that Laurel and Hardy and buildings do not mix. As chimney sweeps, delivery men, builders, or merely as guests, every aspect of the building will conspire to defeat them. Inherently unsympathetic to the chronic clumsiness of Laurel and Hardy, houses turn against them.

In *Safety First* (1923) it is the inherently modern form of the skyscraper that defeats Harold Lloyd. The image in which he dangles from a clock remains one of the most familiar juxtapositions of modern architecture and slapstick acrobatics. In *Entrapment* (1999), the

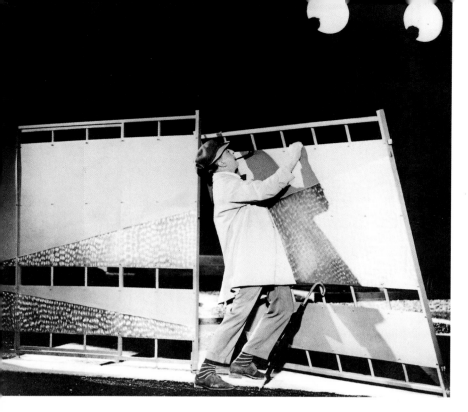

Above
Mon Oncle (Euro London
Films Limited/BFI Stills)

showdown takes place during an escape from the Petronas Towers in Kuala Lumpur. Sean Connery and Catherine Zeta-Jones are seen hanging from the bridge between the two towers (in a more glamorous manner than poor boater-hatted Lloyd), which seem to have been made with films in mind. The baddies have taken over the building, the goodies endeavour to escape the clutches of a high-tech security system. It is a familiar scenario.

In Jacques Tati's 1958 comic masterpiece *Mon Oncle*, Monsieur Hulot, Tati's affectionately drawn, bumbling alter ego, has no difficulty with buildings in the tumbledown, picturesque Parisian suburb in which he lives, but the pretentious Modernist villa of his brother-in-law becomes a forbidding, unsympathetic place in which he becomes an awkward fool.

Mon Oncle is perhaps the most savage cinematic satire on modern architecture, the perfect antidote to the megalomania of Howard Roark, the architect in *The Fountainhead*, which appeared nine years earlier. The scene is set by the film's brilliant opening credits, which appear against a background of a group of dogs sniffing around the dustbins and lamp-posts of a dilapidated Parisian suburb. One of the dogs is wearing a tartan doggy-coat and as it begins to trot off home, the camera, like the other dogs, follows it to its destination – a ridiculous parody of a modern villa in the new part of town where all the houses look the same. While the little domesticated dachshund in the coat is small enough to fit under the gate, the other stray mongrels peer at this bizarre home through a gap in the gate, excluded and bemused.

The film contrasts Hulot's ramshackle house with its convoluted stairs and additions and his brother-in-law's modern villa. In Hulot's world, everything is slow, personal and inefficient; the street sweeper never sweeps, he only chats, market traders sit outside bars and do their business from tables, Hulot reads old newspapers hanging outside the fish stall before they are torn off to wrap the fish. Time passes slowly and has no real meaning, the Protestant work ethic is conspicuous by its absence and the central comedy device is in fact Hulot's unemployability. In the modern villa, every act is assisted by a time-saving device and all the time saved is spent in a kind of painfully awkward boredom. While Hulot's house appears to a soundtrack of ambling Parisian accordion music, the Modernist villa is accompanied only by the disturbing hum of domestic machines. The music disappears as the house appears, and so does the joy and intimacy that characterise the tumbledown Saint-Maur suburb.

The two parts of town are clearly delineated by a kind of no-man's-land, which Hulot and the dogs must cross each time they move between them. A pile of rubble that was once a wall seems to be the result of the onslaught of modernity. As Hulot steps over it, a brick falls out of place. Hulot bends over to pick it up and replaces it in the pile of rubble. Everything in the old part of town has its place and is part of a kind of urban organism that is contrasted with the inorganic harshness of the endless rows of repetitive houses in the new suburb. At one point, the Modernist house becomes an anthropomorphic face looking on disbelievingly at Hulot's clumsiness: its inhabitants appear at its pair of illuminated porthole windows like startled pupils in a pair of shining eyes as Hulot struggles with the automatic gate that he has ruined. The house becomes a reflection of the brother-in-law's equal measures of snobbery, condescension and envy of the ease with which Hulot lives in his own realm. The sterile, antiseptic world of the house (and later of the plastics factory where Hulot is given a job) are the antithesis of the messy, sympathetic square and Hulot's ridiculous flat, which is seen only as a tortuous journey up an illogical set of stairs and landings, a conglomeration of acretions and additions that seems to have grown without design and without the hand of an architect – although it should be noted that it was designed and built especially for the film, implying that Tati's view is a nostalgic idyll that exists more in the fondness of imagination than in the physical city.

Tati went on specifically to target and parody the world of modern architecture in *Playtime* (1967) where he concentrates on public and corporate space rather than the Modernist house. This world of soulless corridors, glass doors and privacy panels creates a ludicrous balletic vision of legs and feet robbed of their bodies, dancing around gaps in the architecture. The film is unequalled in its scathing criticism of the Miesian corporate ideal. (See p 26 for Iain Borden's article on the portrayal of Modernism in Tati's films.)

The themes explored in *Mon Oncle* surface in Czech director Jiri Menzel's film *My Little Village*. Here, the urban planning of the local Communist authority is disrupted by a single house owned by the village idiot, which they have been unable to obtain by moving him into a new housing estate. The village's inhabitants, led by the drunken doctor, attempt to persuade him to stay in the run-down intimate village where he has a place; in the anonymous estate he would be lost, with no friends and with uncaring neighbours. In the end, the chaotic structure of the village wins out against the impersonal luxury of the new blocks.

to look at the broken kitchen window (modern architecture as dangerous enemy) represents the idealism of the society that built these monstrosities with good intentions. Thick skinhead Gary Oldman, sarcastic wide-boy Phil Daniels and dim-witted Tim Roth are the grim reality, the disaffected products of a hostile architectural (as well as social) environment.

The Italian Neo-Realists were among the first to use modern architecture as a kind of cypher for alienation and disenfranchisement, and their work has continued to influence directors, particularly those coming out of England (Ken Loach is the obvious example), who attempt to portray the empty existence of the welfare classes. In Vittorio de Sica's *Bicycle Thieves* (1948), father and son search hopelessly for the lost bike that becomes a symbol of the desperation and impotence

The Italian Neo-Realists were among the first to use modern architecture as a kind of cypher for alienation and disenfranchisement

The results of life in these tower blocks can be seen in Mathieu Kassovitz's *La Haine* (1995), a grim portrayal of the desolate life led by teenagers in concrete blocks that provide no relief from the inevitable unemployment and social deprivation of their inhabitants. The film crew moved into the Parisian housing estate for the duration of the film and the architecture is the single main protagonist: brutally cut and edited, filmed from every angle and shown to a soundtrack blend of rap and Parisian crooning, it is as far away as it is possible to get from the idealised Parisian suburb depicted in *Mon Oncle*. Stanley Kubrick's *A Clockwork Orange* (1971) is set against an equally real backdrop of social engineering: the Thamesmead estate on the edge of east London. Here, the sub-urban housing dream (I hyphenate deliberately) is torn apart as the Modernist dwellings become the perfect soulless backdrop to outrageous violence and thuggery.

Soul-destroying tower blocks have become a stock motif of British film-makers who have built on the harsh realism of the kitchen-sink dramas of the 1950s. Mike Leigh's *Meantime* (1983) is a fine example of the use of drab grey 1960s social housing as a reflection of the short-tempered, hopeless and misanthropic lives of its inhabitants. The hippy social worker who comes

of the working man. The search is set against the blank windows and dumb facades of the new housing project in which they live. It is indicative of this new environment that a man's livelihood could be stolen there, an unimaginable thing in the tiny villages from which most of these protagonists would have emerged in search of escape from grinding rural poverty. The faceless housing becomes the embodiment of hopelessness. The same images of desolate Modernist housing were later used as the background to existentialist angst, inescapable poverty and boredom by Pasolini in *Accattone* (1961) and *Mamma Roma* (1962). Both Fellini and Antonioni used the fascist EUR development in Rome as a symbol of disappointment and banality. In the final scene of Antonioni's *L'Eclisse* (1962) – in which the semi-desolate area represents the film's deeply unfulfilling finale – it is used to particular effect. In *L'Avventura* (1960) he employed an empty modern townscape to suggest the vacuous lives of the central characters, a group of arrogant rich kids. The architecture (the kind of Modernist/classical hybrid that became synonymous with the Mussolini regime) is familiar from the disturbing dreamscapes of de Chirico, an artist who was central in the interpretation of clean, white, modern forms as the setting for a Surreal nightmare world. The existential emptiness, the deep shadows and smooth white surfaces of the soulless modern architecture perfectly mirror the shallowness of the characters' lives.

The diametric contrast (good vs evil) between the homely vernacular and the clinical modern can be seen in the most unexpected of settings. It is present, for example, in George Lucas' *Star Wars* (1977) a film not usually noted for its social commentary. Luke Skywalker's home village is a collection of thick-walled, cosy, rounded huts (based on actual vernacular dwellings in Tunisia), informally grouped in their desert surrounding like a kind of primitive encampment. Darth Vader and his master, however, live on the Death Star, a realisation of the ultimate Modernist dream: an entire planet of modern architecture, no half measures here. The Death Star is a development of the space-station

This employment of architecture to locate us in a past future or alternative world is part of the same identification of modern architecture as the embodiment of everything actually or potentially wrong with society. In Terry Gilliam's *Brazil* (1985), we are presented with a heavily ironic, Orwellian/Kafkaesque vision of the future. An elephantine Art Deco is used to cover up primitive technology in which the duct and the cable are king. The removal of any panel brings forth a spew of gutlike ducts which, like a can of worms, can never be put back in. The gargantuan vulgarity of the pseudo Art Deco can be seen as an ironic commentary on the Postmodernism that was still dominating the world of big-bang corporate architecture at the time

The existential emptiness, the deep shadows and smooth white surfaces of the soulless modern architecture perfectly mirror the shallowness of their lives

fantasy exploited so dramatically in Kubrick's *2001: A Space Odyssey* (1968). In Kubrick's film, the spaceship becomes associated with the menacing HAL, the computer who terrorises the crew and represents the seemingly inevitable consequences of the development of Artificial Intelligence. In *Star Wars* the Death Star represents pure Evil, not tempered by the questions of technology and morality in the more complex *2001*. Naturally, everything on the Death Star is cold and modern, technological and hygienic. In Lucas' prequel, *The Phantom Menace* (1999), the architecture of Naboo (home of the good guys) is a curious quasi-Venetian-Gothic; the design touches an odd blend of Frank Lloyd Wright and Art Nouveau. The lairs of the baddies and the bureaucrats are Futuristic cities; one in particular powerfully recalls the Futuristic vision of *Metropolis*, a planet that is one continuous city. In *The Phantom Menace* little cars hover and fly between enormous towers – just as they do in Luc Besson's *The Fifth Element* (1996). The odd blend of historical styles and almost Roman grandeur (note the Colosseum-like atmosphere of the venue for the pod race) also help to make us aware that we are in a prequel; it is an architecture used to position us in mythical time.

of the film's making. It is an architecture that covers up nasty things about which it is better not to know, a direct parallel with the stick-on detailing of commercial Po-mo at its height. Tim Burton has used similar Art Deco stylings to create his dark, dystopian vision of Gotham City in the Batman films: a gloomy, dense urban setting with cavernous streets bounded by impossibly massive skyscrapers. It is a vision that owes something to New York, to *Metropolis* and to the kind of industrial gloom of *Blade Runner*. In both Gilliam's and Burton's world, the architecture is aggressive and massive, oppressively supporting an unsympathetic vision of a future world governed by ruthless corporations. Very much like 1980s Postmodernism in fact. In *Brazil*, buildings appear as malevolent beings, vomiting forth their guts at any provocation. They are machines for living in that function reluctantly. The modern villa in *Mon Oncle*, too, is categorically a machine for living in. The kitchen cupboards buzz loudly, the fish-shaped fountain (switched on only in honour of important guests and promptly turned off as soon as M Hulot appears) gurgles and cackles, the gate is buzzed open from within. The drone of machines is the soundtrack for this spectacularly uninviting piece of Modernism.

Tati, Gilliam, Antonioni and de Sica all present different visions of an unsympathetic Modernism. What remains at the core of each, though, is the ability of the background to convey not only the mood but the existential emptiness of an uncaring technocratic society. These filmic criticisms of modern architecture stretch back to the beginnings of Modernism itself. The hellish images have even been resurrected as ironic references in an absurd turnaround. The stark buildings with simple punched windows that form the backdrop to the underworld of the proles in *Metropolis* bear a striking resemblance to Rossi's *San Cataldo Cemetery* (1972), while the aesthetic monstrous machine that enslaves them is revived in the buildings of Shin Takamitsu. The Modernist villa parodied in *Mon Oncle* remains a recognisable type. Despite the criticisms, clinical Minimalism and technophile architecture remain popular for those in the trade, while tower blocks are becoming fashionable once more in a kind of post-ironic urban-chic way. In this environment, the categorical acceptance of modern architecture as the enemy, as the embodiment of evil, the de facto style of the villain's lair or the master criminal's penthouse may be coming to a close. Increasingly, as it becomes merely another architectural style from which to choose, or as it becomes more acceptable to the broader public and less tinged by association with the epic and visible disasters of modern planning and design, Modernism may yet become one of the good guys – but it will have to overcome the effects of a substantial filmic legacy that will continue to testify eloquently to its many failures. △

Material

Jacques Tati and
Modern Architecture

Inhabited by the clumsy, comic figure of Monsieur Hulot, Jacques Tati's films
are generally assumed to be a critique of Modernism. Through an investigation
of the materiality of architecture and sound in *Playtime*, Iain Borden not
only contests this popular misconception but shows how Tati expressly
explored modern architecture's comic and pleasurable potential. This offers
an invaluable insight into the experiential, which Borden shows has much
to offer contemporary Modernists.

Sounds

Jean-Luc Godard's classic film *Alphaville* (1965) is the canonical portrayal of the dystopian state and its mechanistic city. Shot on location in Paris, it depicts a world of disembodied, computerised voices, flashing signals, directive arrows, tall towers, dark streets and fluorescent interiors; as a sign announces, it is an urbanism of 'silence, logic security, prudence'.

This correlation of Modernism and the state was common in the 1950s and 1960s, and provides much of the context for the second of Jacques Tati's films to feature his famous invention, Monsieur Hulot. In *Mon Oncle* (1958, production design Henri Schmitt), the chaplinesque Hulot lives stooped under the eaves of a ramshackle tenement building of *vieux* Saint-Maur, in a fast-disappearing France replete with market, mischievous boys, chattering residents, cafés and horse-drawn carts. It is dirty, haphazard, old. By contrast, Hulot's sister Mme Arpel and her husband live in a different, highly bourgeois part of town (filmed in Créteil), with flat-roofed house, geometric garden, streamlined car, industrialised gadgets and suburban routines. It is hygienic, planned, modern.

Hulot moves between these two worlds, which are separated by a decrepit stone wall and freshly laid road. Not for him, though, the new Saint-Maur of modern school, chic restaurants, speeding traffic, plastic flowers ('flowers that last'), clean factories and

rectilinear apartments; despite the improving efforts of his relatives, Hulot continually returns to old Saint-Maur by *cyclomoteur*. In the Arpels' eyes, Hulot is an embarrassing under-achiever unable to find his place in modernised France, and must be kept away from their son.

One might expect *Playtime* (1967, production design Eugène Roman), Tati's third film featuring Hulot, to exhibit similar preoccupations regarding the alienating nature of the modern city. In 1964, to shoot *Playtime*, he constructed a giant set on wasteland near Vincennes outside Paris, a 162,000 square-foot downscaled pseudocity that ate up 65,000 cubic yards of concrete, 42,300 square feet of plastic, 34,200 square feet of timber and 12,600 square feet of glass. It was quickly nicknamed 'Tativille'. As Tati himself described it, the set was 'the real star of the film', displaying a Paris comprised almost entirely of rectilinear glass, steel and concrete architecture, directly based on the Esso building at La Défense (1963) and implicitly on Lever House (1952) in New York.[1] Resolutely modern, Tativille is stripped of the history, memory, colours, dirt, nature, family and other aspects of old France still visible in *Mon Oncle*; it is a city in which Hulot bumbles around from faltering business errand to unrequited *amour*. Unsurprisingly, given this setting, *Playtime* is commonly interpreted as an assault on Modernism, a more playful counterpart to *Alphaville*.

However, it was not Modernist architecture in itself that Tati found repellent. As he stated, 'if I had been against modern architecture I would have shown the most ugly buildings' Instead, Tati made Tativille 'so that no architect could say anything against it. I took the finest I could. These buildings are beautiful'. Similarly, when accused of attacking modern kitchens while many had none at all, Tati retorted that he was not criticising kitchens per se, only consumerist society.[2] In this light, his films are not so much 'shots at modern architecture', as Andrea Kahn states, but shots within modern architecture. Furthermore, I contend, they are overtly positive attempts to reassert the poetic aspects of modern life that are latent within Modernist urbanism. In short, Tati's films help unlock the experiential and comic potential of modern architecture.

Comic Democracy

Playtime, as is often noted, is in the tradition of Charlie Chaplin's *Modern Times*, (1936), criticising urban rationalism through the mode of comedy wherein a seemingly hopeless character triumphs at the end. Certainly there are parallels between Hulot and Chaplin, but where Chaplin's creation is clownish, actively

disruptive of the regimented institutions and pompous individuals he encounters, Tati's is far more passive yet pervasive. He is called Monsieur Hulot, but we never learn his first name; he is recognised in the street, but also mistaken for others just as others are mistaken for him; he is usually ignored. In *Playtime*, Hulot is not the 'star' of the movie, merely the most apparent of many characters. He is each and every one of us, central yet peripheral to the city.

To Hulot, 'the son of the air and of the wind',[3] life simply happens as he circulates around town, occasionally provoking disorder (as when a Hulot look-alike causes M Giffard to bash his nose into a glass door), but generally just creating fun from within. For example, in *Les vacances de monsieur Hulot* (1953), the first of Tati's Hulot films, an earnest male suitor impresses on the bored-looking Martine that, 'it is the duty of the politically conscious woman to play a more important role in exposing the decadence of the middle cl ...', while Hulot, searching for a ping-pong ball, is unknowingly disrupting two card games, later leading to volatile allegations of cheating. There is, then, a politics here, but not as overt assertion, for in Tati's films it is the dispersed nature of the humour that provides critical and hence radical qualities. This is an everyday humour of 'comic democracy',[4] where everyone has a right to be silly and ridiculous, to have fun and laugh.

The same is true of Tati's comic critique of architecture. He described his intentions as being simply to bring 'a little smile'[5] to Modernist architecture: architecture and the city are given the right to a comic mode – a lighter and more humorous way to be experienced, quite distinct from art gallery reverence. If architecture is everywhere around us, so too, necessarily, is humour. Tati's humorous moments suggest that all architectural scenes, whether in Tativille or the street outside, have such comic potential if only we would pay enough attention to realise it. To explore this territory, I focus here on one particular aspect of Tati's cinematic inventions: the sound of architecture.[6]

Soundscape

If Tativille deals with the immateriality of glass and space, it also involves sound, for *Playtime* not only has a visual landscape but also a highly sophisticated aural landscape, a *paysage sonore*.[7]

Film, even 'silent' film accompanied by music and live interpretation, has always been an auditory production. In *Playtime*, this is sound of a very particular kind. Tati combines music (by Francis Lemarque, James Campbell and David Stein) with multilanguage dialogue (much of it barely comprehensible) and closely microphoned details that are frequently foregrounded on the aural stage. By contrast, there is little of the background, obfuscating rumble of the city. As such, *Playtime*'s soundscape, originally recorded by sound director Jacques Maumont on to five stereophonic tracks, bears comparison with *musique concrète*. Pioneered by French sound technician Pierre Schaeffer and taken up by composers like Karlheinz Stockhausen, who worked on his seminal Etude in Paris in the early 1950s, concrete music offers an urbanised construction variously composed from 'real' and synthesised sounds, white noise, feedback, chance operations and improvised performances.

The composition that results in *Playtime* has no real keynote (a base tone against which other sounds are modulated) other than the babbling dialogue of different European languages. Yet, as with concrete music, what may first seem like chaos is in *Playtime* a highly ordered composition. The low ambient level renders a resolutely hi-fi rather than lo-fi quality, in which distinct sounds and, hence, social as well as aural effects are identifiable.

The most obvious sound in *Playtime* is that which gives identity to people. Footsteps, opening doors and other actions are all carefully recorded to generate a sonic presence for each individual – in *Les vacances*, for example, it is Hulot's rambunctiously misfiring car that first announces his arrival. Above all, in *Playtime* there is dialogue – not the quick-fire repartee, logical conversation or tense argument of conventional films, but a continual yet frequently unintelligible set of phrases and exchanges, often conducted in more than one language. As Michel Chion notes, the effect is like European beaches, where sun worshippers from countless countries create an international mixture, all curiously estranged from each other.[8]

Sound also gives identity to particular spaces. In the opening scene, it is the languid pronouncements of flight information, quickly followed by the roar of jets, that first define the location as an airport. Similarly, throughout the events set in the office building of Giffard (whom Hulot is unsuccessfully trying to meet) the stern mood of the architecture is subtly augmented by barely audible electronic humming and buzzes.

At other times, it is the separation of space that is emphasised. For example, when outside the Giffard/Schneider apartment building, we are aware from movements and gesticulations that the residents are speaking and that the television is on, while we hear nothing except for the occasional passing car. Sound, or its absence, divides one space (apartment interior) from another (street exterior), while this very separation simultaneously highlights the visual connection of the two, and questions what is inside and out, private and public. In a yet more complex variant, sound at once identifies, separates and unifies the different parts of Tativille. Notably, the female announcer first heard in the airport is also evident in the Salon des Arts Ménagers and hotel foyer, telling us we are in a particular kind of building while emphasising homogeneity across these spaces.

If space can be demarcated by sound, it can also be intensified. For example, echo is often cited by phenomenologists as a measurement of architectural space, yielding a sense of size and scale. However, such formulations tend to stress the 'timeless task of architecture' to provide a structure between the universality of its space-types – the ruin, cave, cavern house – and the equally universal subject, man.[9] By contrast, echo is almost entirely absent from Tativille, where sound stresses the very specificity of space and person that phenomenology tends to erase. In the office waiting room scene, it is Hulot who fidgets and rustles, makes rushes of air as he sits down on modern chairs and squeaks as he moves across the hard floor. As a result, the waiting room becomes more like a waiting room, and Hulot more like a person waiting.

Implicit here is an important aspect of soundscapes: that it is not just sound itself – the sound event – that reworks architecture, but the way people perceive sound, the auditory event. Whereas vision tends to place us at the margin of a space, where we notice only what happens in front of our eyes, sound tends to place us at the centre, where we become more aware of what is happening all around. In addition, sound tends to make us more participatory – a condition noted by a range of urban commentators, from geographer Paul Rodaway to architectural theorist Juhani Pallasmaa:

> Sight makes us solitary, whereas hearing creates a sense of connection and solidarity. We stare alone at the suspense of the circus, but the burst of applause after the relaxation of suspense unites us to the crowd.[10]

Garden, this is a soundmark, an aural landmark, used to denote a shared conception of community, in this case, rural France. A cockerel in the heart of Tativille is then an absurd comic intrusion of the countryside into the city, challenging the boundary between urban and rural.

As this suggests, Playtime's treatment of sound is not entirely logical, and when observing Tativille we often clearly hear distant things as if they were nearby. At other times, steps and other sounds conflict with what is seen on the screen; in one airport shot several different people walk along, including a man delivering flowers, none of whose movements correspond to some curiously sucking footsteps that dominate the sound stage, only to fade away for no apparent reason.

Sometimes, this illogicality of sound occurs within a sound field (the sound made by a single source), as when the door in which Barbara sees a reflection of the Eiffel Tower emits a wholly inappropriate low-pitched and muted boom. In a more spatialised example, when Giffard advances along the corridor towards the waiting Hulot, his footsteps get louder, yet only after fluctuating in volume; while their rhythm stays constant, reaffirming the presence of a human body,

Sound divides the interior from the exterior. This separation highlights the visual connection of private and public, inside and out.

For example, towards the start of Playtime, Hulot, while high up on a building terrace, is attracted by two 'sound signals', a car horn and police whistle. Here, the visual regime of architecture is disrupted by a noise that does not conform to what can be seen, encouraging Hulot to do something different: he looks downwards to street level, where Barbara (the main female character, later befriended by Hulot) and her fellow tourists are arriving at the same building. And although Hulot and Barbara do not meet, remaining unaware of each other, the sound signal nonetheless joins them momentarily. Here, sound is subversive, flowing outside the bounded visual system imposed by architecture, causing people to do things and to create possibilities.

The effect, particularly as the aural city often changes more rapidly than the visual city, is to impose a different rhythm on to the visual and physical rhythm of the city, leading in turn to layering, interweaving and discontinuity, as when sound transgresses barriers. For example, when a cockerel crows at dawn outside the Royal

their varying loudness challenges both the position of the body and the length, linearity and aural qualities of the corridor. Tati here disrupts the dialectic of sight and sound, oscillating sound while allowing visual information to proceed linearly. One rhythm is out of synchronisation with another.

At other times the discontinuity is within a soundscape (formed by a multiplicity of different soundfields). For example, Tati often switches levels in two or more speakers' dialogue, making one suddenly much louder (an effect achieved by postsynchronising the dialogue, and recording it very close-up). Alternatively several people can be clearly heard, but only as a mumble, with odd phrases floating to the foreground; snatches of conversation like 'I feel at home everywhere I go', 'I hope my daughter writes', 'Do you remember the guide in Amsterdam?' are all audible in one scene, but without any connecting interaction. Meaningless in context, these are what Chion calls 'memory burps',[11] aural fragments of other lives and histories that bubble on to the surface of Tativille, recalling Walter Benjamin's assertion that 'the past can be seized only as an image which flashes up at the instant when it can be recognized and is never

Footnotes
1. *Home Ludens: an Analysis of Four Films by Jacques Tati*, Lucy Fischer, PhD thesis, New York University, 1978, cited in *Design Book Review*, 'Playtime with Architects', no. 24, Spring 1992, p 23; and *Cinema and Architecture Méliès, Mallet-Stevens, Multimedia*, 'Architecture in the Films of Jacques Tati', François Penz, British Film Institute, London, 1997, pp 64–65.
2. *Les cahiers du cinéma*, 'Le Champ large', JA Fieschi and J Narboni, no. 199, March

1968; and *Le cinéma français des années 60*, Freddy Bruache, Five Continents, Paris, 1987, pp 17–18, cited in 'Jacques Tati, Witness of Modernism', Léonard Hamburger, course essay, MSc Archietctural History, The Bartlett (University College London), 1997.
3. *Les vacances de monsieur Hulot*, Jacques Kermabon, Yellow Now, Crisnes, 1988, cited in Hamburger, 'Jacques Tati, Witness of Modernism'.
4. *The Films of Jacques Tati*, Michel Chion, Guernica (Toronto), 1997, pp 20–40.
5. *Le Champ large*, Fieschi and Narboni
6. For an extended version of this article see *The Hieroglyphics of the City*, Neil Leach (ed), 'Architecture's Playtime: The Pleasures of City Modernism in the Films of Jacques Tati', Iain Borden, Routledge (London), 2000.
7. *Sensuous Geograhies: Body, Sense and Place*, 'Auditory Geographies', Paul Rodaway, Routledge (London), 1994, pp 82–113.
8. *Films of Jacques Tati*, Chion, p 65.
9. *Architecture + Urbanism*, 'An Architecture of the Seven Seas', Juhani Pallasmaa, July 1994, pp 30–31 and 37.
10. Ibid, p 31.
11. *Films of Jacques Tati*, Chion, p 59.
12. *Illuminations*, 'Theses on the Philosophy of History', Walter Benjamin, Schocken Books (New York), 1969, p 255.
13. '*Playtime* by Jacques Tati', Jung Hee Lee, course essay, MSc Architectural History, The Bartlett (University College London), 1997.
14. *Films of Jacques Tati*, Chion, pp 128–129.
15. *Brecht on Theatre*, 'The Street Scene', Bertolt Brecht, J Willet (ed), Methuen, London, 1978, p 126 and cited in *Critique of Everyday Life. Volume 1: Introduction*, Henri Lefebvre, Verso (London), 1991, p 14.
16. *Les cahiers du cinéma*, Jacques Tati interview, no. 303, September 1979, cited in 'Jacques Tati, Witness of Modernism', Hamburger.
17. *Qu'est-ce le cinéma*, André Bazin, Éditions du Cerf, Paris, 1975, p 43, quoted in *Films of Jacques Tati*, Chion, p 48.
18. *Critique of Everyday Life*, Lefebvre, p 64.
19. see in particular: *Modernism and Modernization in Architecture*, Helen Castle (ed), Academy Editions (London), 1999.
20. 'Phenomenal Zones', 'Questions of Perception: Phenomenology of Archietcture', p 55.
21. *Fast Cars, Clean Bodies: Decolonization and the Reordering of French Culture*, Kristin Roff, MIT (Cambridge, Mass), 1995, p 5.

seen again'.[12] Sound is one way in which other worlds and other lives infiltrate Tativille.

Because the logic of Tativille's soundscape is frequently disrupted, it has to be reconfigured by the audience. One part of this operation is to realise consciously that all sounds are sounds of action. For a person, the sound comes from speaking to someone, walking on something, sitting on a chair. For a thing, sound comes from a chair being moved, a floor being walked upon, an engine running. Thus in the waiting room scene, Hulot's body acts as a mediator between the chairs, flooring and the room volume, a process revealed to us by a sequence of sounds.[13] Tati's obsession with immobile sounds – sounds which do not track across the screen – emphasises this effect; rather than a movement, they emphasise a particular place and source. Everything, as Chion notes, is a *grelot*, a small bell that we hang up to notify our presence. Sound is hooked on to something.[14]

The movement of sound in Tativille is mostly compositional, where one sound interacts with another. For example, in the office waiting room, Hulot's footsteps, brushes, gusts and scrapes are punctuated by periods of silence. Furthermore, these sounds are juxtaposed with the other waiting man who, in contrast to the erratic Hulot, precisely opens his briefcase, extracts a document and pen, makes notes, and then replaces his accoutrements, creating a highly detailed series of noises that runs: brush, crick, zip, sniff, brush, flick, click, tap, click, clap, zip, sniff, steps [and exit].

The rhythms of sound in Tativille formulate a poetic composition of dialogue, footsteps, scrapes, clashes and quietude. Furthermore, these are rhythms that conjoin with other rhythms in the film – visual, comedic, narrative, spatial – to create a complex rhythm-world where each element has its own life, yet also feeds off all others. This soundscape is a cumulative, mutating and experiential entity, requiring people for its production and reception.

This is not, therefore, a soundscape in the manner of a comprehensive street map. Nor is it a set of objects, where sound events exist in their own right. Rather than simply reading the city by looking at it, Tativille suggests a sonorous engagement between people and architecture; along with being spectators of architecture we could also recover its auditory aspects, becoming its audience (from the Latin *audire*, to hear). Tativille indicates how we might do this, and so learn to participate in the *musique concrète* of the city.

Modernity

Tativille is not a place apart, but a parallel world where city life is turned up a notch on the dial. Just as Brecht's epic theatre sought its basic model in the traffic accident and street corner,[15] so in *Playtime* Tati set out to portray everyday life just as it was. He was delighted when a 14-year-old remarked that when he left the movie theatre the street outside had exactly the same architecture, people and behaviour as the film.[16] In this respect, Tati was once again working in an old cinematic tradition, where prenarrative films recorded not only important historical events like coronations and state funerals but also everyday street scenes, workplaces and leisure.

After *Les vacances*, Hulot was described by French film critic André Bazin as someone who seemed 'not to dare to wholly exist',[17] while in *Mon Oncle*, he is cast spatially and socially apart from the bourgeois modernism of his relatives. In *Playtime*, however, Hulot has moved on within the modern world, existing no longer apart from, but through, the city; he is perhaps even representative of the birth of the new metropolitan individual, 'bursting forth in all his beauty and undeniable authenticity', who revels in the pleasures and opportunities of the city.[18]

This is a place of reflections, visions – a place of modern and material delights

What does this mean for Modernism today? While there is a renewed interest in Modernism – as architecture from Norman Foster to Claudio Silvestrin, retro furniture designs from Bertoia to Panton, restaurants and shops from Wagamama to Ikea, and magazines from the *Architectural Review* to *Elle Decoration*, *Living etc* and *Wallpaper** show[19] – too often this Modernism is constrained to matters of visualisation, forms and surfaces. Hence the phenomenologist counter-reactions of those like Stephen Holl and Juhani Pallasmaa, who call for 'movement between the absolutes of architectural intention and the indefinite urban assemblage' and for 'an understanding of alternative ways of moving through cities'.[20] *Playtime* shows how this might happen, as a Modernism of friendships, amusement, pleasure and gentle love. This is a place of reflections, visions, utterances, noises, rhythms, journeys, exchanges – a place of modern and material delights. Kristin Ross, studying postwar French culture, identified in Tati's films an architectural world that 'tended to dictate to people their gestures and movements'.[21] But what I see in *Playtime* is a myriad possibilities and pleasures. ᗄ

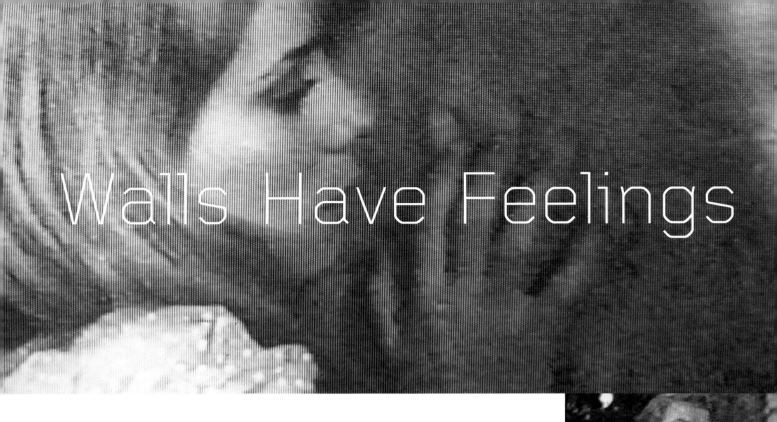

Walls Have Feelings

Cult Films about Sex in 1960s London

Katherine Shonfield proposes that to understand what film tells us about architecture one must look at where it is conspicuously absent as a subject – to what cinema does best: love and romance. She discusses how the boundaries between urban territories are dissolved architecturally and sexually in two films made in 1960s London, Roman Polanski's *Repulsion* and the Michael Caine vehicle *Alfie*. Shonfield argues that in these films, made in a period of sociosexual revolution, the dissolution of the wall acts as an analogy for the sexual penetration of the female body.

THE MODERN DWELLING

Architects seem to demand very particular things of film. We ask it to give us a great picture of a great building – so we like the way *Wings of Desire* shows off Scharoun's State Library. Or we like it to reflect back to us a familiar image of a great architect – Frank Lloyd Wright in *The Fountainhead* (1949). Or we enjoy the way film pays yet more homage to the importance of our profession by presenting back to us our own visions of the future – as in Terry Gilliam's *Brazil* (1985) or Ridley Scott's *Blade Runner* (1982).

In this way, we read in film a reflection of what we already know. The paradox I want to propose is that to understand what film can tell us about architecture, we need to look in the place where the overt subject 'architecture' is absent. Instead, we have to look where the subject is what film does best, and that is sex and romance.

It is part of the paradox that architecture is, in quite a profound sense, the subject of nearly all feature films. Architecture frames the story film tells: indeed, it is far more important to film than to that other great purveyor of narrative, the novel. In the novel, the reader is involved through the description of the characters' innermost thoughts. But in film, as in our experience of everyday life, you can't hear what people think – or, as in Woody Allen's *Annie Hall* (1977), the expression of thoughts is mannered and awkward. Film, that medium of unique visual intimacy, understands the interiority of its characters primarily through visual clues. It uses architecture, and in particular the space of the city, to carry its metaphors and commentaries on the characters and the psychological and social – as well as the physical – context in which they dwell. In performing this multiple role, film can often be more precise about architect's material and technical possibilities (and pitfalls) than the technical literature itself.

Here, I want to explore what film can tell us about architecture and the city, and their intertwinings, at a specific time and in a specific place. The time is the 1960s; the place London. The 1960s was both a great period for British film and a decisive moment in the modernisation of London, when more building was initiated than at any time before. Both of the films at which I will look – Roman Polanski's *Repulsion* (1965) and Lewis Gilbert's *Alfie* (1966) – were released in the middle of the decade when the so-called sexual revolution was enabled by the technology of the contraceptive pill. The pill called into question, for the first

time, a fundamental distinction between inside and outside, allowing a blurring of spatial understanding at the most personal, intimate level. This blurring is paralleled in architecture by its apparent opposite: a growing preoccupation with the definition of the edge between components, and between categories. In the short heyday of system building in housing, there is a concurrent architectural paradox. In the need to define the edge between components precisely enough for system building, one ends up smearing the same fundamental border as the contraceptive pill did. That smeared border is the edge between inside and outside. If the wall is essentially a singular element to be hauled into place, then inside inevitably becomes the same as outside. It is no longer another, distinct place; it is merely the other side of the wall.

A further paradox is that for the line to remain crisp and distinct, and to maintain the security of the interior against water penetration, you need sealants. Sealants, in particular mastics, are gooey and viscous: they have the potential to distort and smear the very edges you are trying to maintain intact.

An unlikely source of technical commentary is found in *Repulsion*. Unstable but beautiful Carol, played by Catherine Deneuve, works in a beauty salon in South Kensington, a cosmopolitan district in south-west London. Her work involves smearing impasto face-packs over her ageing customers' cracks. She is depicted as a fragile, introverted virgin: her beauty attracts a slightly awed response from her boyfriend. Her sister's departure for a week in Rome, with an insensitive, would-be playboy, provides the opportunity for Carol's fears of penetration to be played out, both in the city and in the body of her flat. The surfaces of the flat start to crack, no longer holding back the outside, and at the climax of the film the walls themselves begin literally to smear the edge between Carol and themselves.

If system building carries the fantasy that an interior is just the other side of the wall, *Repulsion* is the story of the interior's revenge. Carol's fears are focused on the questionable integrity of the walls of her apartment, manifested in the form of a damp patch. These walls – unsponsored by either of the Royal Institutes, of Chartered Surveyors or Architects – are nevertheless remarkable in that they explicitly demonstrate three types of constructed failure associated with contemporary changes in building practice in postwar London. Damp penetration, cracking of internal surfaces and failure of mastic sealants all come under the microscope eye of Carol's technical inspection.

Damp provokes an extreme form of fungal growth; what is latent and alien inside is released as if the wall were Pandora's. The eventual universal adoption of cavity wall construction in postwar Britain led to the perception of a literal gap in the market: the space

Opposite top and above
Repulsion
(Euro London Films Limited)

Opposite bottom
Alfie (Paramount)

Above top
Coventry Tile Hill (Architectural
Review, 1956, p 29)

Above top
Lasto-meric: The Thiokol
Seal of Security and the
Tremco Representative
(*Architectural Record*,
December 1967, p 176)

Above middle
Suwide Tedlar plastic wall
covering (*Architects Journal*,
13th July 1966)

Above bottom images
Repulsion
(Euro London Films Limited)

Opposite top left and middle
Alfie (Paramount)

Opposite top right
Repulsion
(Euro London Films Limited)

Opposite bottom
Ministry of Housing and
Local Government Homes
of Today and Tomorrow,
diagrams by Gordon Cullen,
HMSO London 1961

within the wall. Until revealed as carcinogenic, pumped formaldehyde insulation was marketed by door-to-door salesmen with the tag that it would reduce heating bills. From the mid-1960s it became increasingly likely that a wall might contain an alien viscous substance unseen within its apparent traditionally built solidity. Like the sprouting wall in *Repulsion*, the formaldehyde insulation emerged from its solidity in the form of toxic fumes to attack the occupants of the spaces beyond. Invading services prove too much for the integrity of internal plaster skin: it is ruptured, and a massive crack instantly appears.

Carol flings herself against the wall as a haven of security in the face of the threats within her apartment. She clings to it; and it begins to cling to her. She finds it melting beneath her fingertips. The wall itself acts like a monstrous mastic joint: it returns to a state of viscosity. In the words of an examination of mastic joint failure in 1967 the 'presence of moisture behind the brick wall causes "reversion" of sealant'.[1]

During a dream scene, Carol seals off her bedroom by dragging a wardrobe to block the doorway. Penetration of this blockade is signalled at first by a light, and then by a man who breaks his way in. At the threshold of any breach to the membrane of Carol's physical security, Polanski places either a man or the threat of one. *Repulsion* reverses the parallel fiction of the world of building-product literature. There, an uncompromisingly male figure accompanies and confirms the very security he undermines in Carol's nightmare of building failure. The language of security particularly characterises the marketing of sealants. It is as if the industry instinctively recognises the risks of the pared down inflexible forms of construction that have become the postwar norm: the sealant is portrayed with a masculine sense of responsibility, sole guardian of the integrity of the interiors.

The form and language associated with the mastic gun, the appliance that was in general use for the application of mastic by the late 1950s, expresses the unease with which the increasingly inflexible, component-based building industry viewed this viscous product. A glossary of sealant and glazing terms, published in *Architectural Record* in 1968,[2] tells us that mastic may be made up to 'gun consistency', a 'compound made up to a degree of softness suitable for application through the nozzle of a caulking gun'; and 'knife consistency', a 'compound formulated

in a degree of firmness suitable for application with a glazing knife'. The finishes seek to deny the viscosity, the smearing qualities of the product, and present its finished form, through the language of violent defence (knives and guns), as something uncompromisingly protective.

By contrast, the woman washing graffiti from the *Suwide Tedlar* plastic wall covering wears a diaphanous, nightie-like garment, no gloves, and is lit, as if by Polanski, so that her individual features are wiped out. She is apparently as distracted by the surface of the wall as *Repulsion*'s heroine herself.

According to the glossary, the conditions to which the mastic compound is subject when left to its own devices tell a story of feminine, defenceless weakness, equivalent to that of Catherine Deneuve's character left alone within her flat. The language combines the technical terminology of the beauty salon where Carol works as an assistant, holding back failures of the body's external skin, with the signifiers of feminine sensibility: 'Wrinkling – the formulation of wrinkles on the skin of a compound during the formation of its surface skin by oxidisation'; 'Weeping – failure to support its own weight in a joint, but less pronounced than sagging'; 'Shrinking – deficiency of a compound, when it occurs excessively, in which the applied bead loses volume and contracts'; and, of course, 'Bleeding – the absortion of oil or vehicle in compound into an adjacent porous surface'.[3]

The pathetic incapacity of mastic to function without a controlling male containment is paralleled by the depiction of women in contemporary building-product literature, echoing uncannily the hesitant and fragile form of Deneuve's depiction of Carol.

For Carol, the outside territory of London simply extends and varies the assault on her edges that happens inside her flat. She takes to the streets of London when it is at its most exhibitionist. In 1965 it has the eyes of the Western world on it: it is dubbed 'the swinging city' by *Time* magazine. For Carol, traversing the streets of London is an ordeal where she must unavoidably face the visual intrusion of another's eyes. She mainly looks down, to a cracking pavement, which menacingly suggests a grotesque, underground world beyond. As with the besieged borders to her flat, the perforation of her edges by city civilisation is heralded by a male. She goes over and over the same ground: the traffic island opposite South Kensington underground station. She has to run the traditional gauntlet of the guardians of the road surface – the men who are digging it up. In this sequence, Polanksi puts us as nearly as he can inside the body of Carol, experiencing the penetrative look of a man so at ease in the streets that he can afford to be completely static.

We watch her back and her inclined head as she crosses the road with the workman's hut in the centre of the frame: his torso and then his face and then a close-up come into view, seen through Carol's eyes. Just as she is passing he mutters, 'Fancy a bit of the other, darling?' and the relaxed face of another workman, seated and staring calmly at Carol, also hoves into view. The final shot shows the first workman leering directly into the camera.

the landscapes of the remodelled modern city to its electrical appliances – with promiscuous freedom.

Like his forebear Don Giovanni, Alfie's exploits depend on an absence of communication between the women themselves. He needs them to be predictably fixed in space, a prerequisite that allows him to dart with impunity around the city sampling Woman as a kind of static community, akin to the objects in the diagrams, as he miraculously dissolves walls and enters where, and whenever, he wants.

Repulsion and *Alfie* reveal a moment of confident appropriation of the city at large, and its female inhabitants, as legitimate territory for the male sexual adventurer

His pose is mirrored by Alfie's in the film of the same name, released the year after *Repulsion*. Both of these films reveal a moment of confident appropriation of the city at large, and its female inhabitants, as legitimate territory for the male sexual adventurer. This moment is particularly remarkable: the *flâneur*, Baudelaire's archetypal urban drifter of the 19th century, now so commands the streets that he can sit or lounge in them, just as if they were his own living room. In its opening shots, *Alfie* makes this appropriation of London explicit.

Alfie addresses the camera face on, directly from the South Bank: his backdrop is the Houses of Parliament. He is possessing the city – London – via its architectural symbiosis, and with all the authority of a Member of Parliament called upon to comment on his specialist subject for the 'Nine O'Clock News': in Alfie's case, London 'birds'.

He plays out an architectural fantasy embodied in the series of diagrams, familiar to architects working in Britain at the time, from the Ministry of Housing and Local Government's 'Homes of Today and Tomorrow', which stipulated space standards in new housing. In the diagrams, the city is a domain of fixed objects, generically similar. They are matter-of-fact, mass-produced, clear in both their edges and their purpose, without mystery. There is no interior as we know it: as implied by system building this is in effect dissolved along with that familiar distinction between outside and inside. Through this domain the flow – the arrow-headed swirls of the ministry diagrams – can penetrate, unhindered by the edge, the largest and the smallest objects, from

At the threshold of each conquest, Alfie addresses his admiring spectator face on, smirking: irrespective of whether he is inside or outside the building. Popping in and out at will, Alfie turns the new high-rise into one more object presented for penetration. In postwar London, as in the ministry's diagrams, scale is no barrier to Alfie, the nimble arrow. His Don Giovanni conquests are aided by his very own Leporello, in the form of the new building materials that transform the experience of wandering through the city.

Alfie walks down a traditional London street past typical shop frontages that can only be negotiated via complex sets of thresholds. Looking for an opportunity, he comes across the new plate-glass window of a modern-style dry-cleaner. It is the thinnest possible, most transparent, wall – and yet it is still a wall, and provokes an intricate dance with the assistant on the other side around the theme of inside, outside and not quite either: he knocks on the window, she turns round, they play at touching with the glass wall in between. Alfie, arrowlike, imperceptibly slips in and turns the 'open' sign to 'closed'. The transformation of public to private achieved with the minimum of architectural interference.

These films, ostensibly concerned with sex, reveal preoccupations with the wall. Both the divider between inside and outside that architects worry about – and the walls of the body – in the case of both films, the woman's body. In *Alfie* and *Repulsion* the dissolution of the wall – through entry or otherwise – works as an analogy for the sexual penetration of the body, the dissolution of the body's edges. On a wider scale, modernised postwar London is seen as a territory where man may roam freely. So the borders between urban territories, between inside and outside, are dissolved both architecturally and sexually. ◿

Footnotes
1. *Architectural Record*, May 1968, p 207.
2. Ibid, p 210.
3. *Architectural Record*, op cit.

Evil Residence

The House and
the Horror Film

Here, Bob Fear deconstructs four contemporary horror films
– *Poltergeist*, *Amityville Horror*, *Hellraiser* and *Candyman* –
to discover how various types of everyday, domestic
architectures become important narrative devices in these
stories. The suburban des-res, the dream country home
and the trendy apartment all come alive with evil intent –
to expose and manipulate dysfunctional family and community
relationships.

The greatest horror stories are those that subvert the familiar. Our nightmares are usually constructed from aspects of the immediate domestic environment – all hell breaks lose in the living room; a monster hides under the bed waiting to pounce on us in our sleep; a masked murderer comes to inspect the plumbing just when we're in the shower; and the devil drops by to possess our little sister. Our homes are our castles and when they are invaded what sanctuary do we have left? Fear of losing our basic security and comfort is a paranoia we do our best to subdue, so it is inevitable that horror films, from the German Expressionist *The Cabinet of Dr Caligari* (1919) and *Nosferatu* (1922) to Hollywood's *Scream* series (1996-97), has done its best to exploit those fears that are common to all of us. We seem to enjoy the adrenaline rush of fright.

To a child, home and family are the whole world. Many of Steven Spielberg's films have

body like a doll; pinning her, undignified, to the ceiling. However, this only fuels her determination and gives her the strength to fight back. One of the best moments in the film is where Spielberg has her running through the obligatory nightmare-treacle (seen more literally in Wes Craven's *A Nightmare on Elm Street*) and subjects her to a Hitchcockian pull-back/zoom-in camera trick which extends the length of the corridor whilst keeping her in the same spot in the foreground. 'Leave my babies alone!' screaming, she manages to outrun the illusion, reach the kids' bedroom and once again literally claw them back to safety from the all-engulfing entity threatening to suck them into the closet.

Spielberg paints his ideal family portrait in a setting of suburban paradise. We see row upon row of well-tended, immaculate, detached, double-garaged houses, complete with kids playing on the streets, dad watching the game on the TV, mom tidying away the kids' clothes. But by the end of the film, the Freeling family has become solitary in suburbia. Diane's calls for help over the garden fence go unheeded because of the family's

been successes because he has never forgotten what it's like to be a child and has tapped into that part of us all that can never forget those childhood nightmares. In 1982's *Poltergeist*, Spielberg practises his stock trademark of presenting peaceful family bliss in the suburbs before letting loose the aliens/ghosts/sharks. In this film there really is something under the bed and there most definitely is a monster in the closet. The evil that erupts into this 2.4-children-plus-dog household threatens to pull it apart. It uses Robbie's irrational paranoia about the kinetic ability of an ancient, dead tree in the garden as a distraction, whilst kidnapping Carole-Anne – the naïve, youngest and most vulnerable child. This causes the Robbie to flip and stay at a friend's house whilst testing the parents' sanity to its limit. Taking advantage of dad's scepticism and two-dimensional thinking the monster nearly prevents the indomitable strength of a mother's love from clawing back her child from the jaws of evil on 'the other side' of the closet, back to normality and safety.

But the house/monster doesn't give in without a fight. It uses the cheap trick of teasing up Diane's – mom's – T-shirt as she lies on her bed, showing her underwear and flipping her

inability to adhere to neighbourly social graces. Spielberg hints at this earlier when the Freelings alienate their neighbour by turning up in hysterics on his doorstep, trying to describe their experiences of moving furniture and trembling foundations, but ultimately unable to do so convincingly. Thus the family is trapped in their paradise; our desire to build our garden walls high and protect ourselves from the outside world can also be to our detriment. The Freeling castle begins to crumble and tries to take the family with it. The film becomes an indictment of modern living. The father is employed by the company that built and sells the houses, demonstrating to prospective buyers the fashionable, sophisticated features of these desirable residences. He learns that the company built the entire development on ancient native North American burial grounds removing the headstones but leaving the bodies. Thus our desire for the ultimate in luxury and convenience, our own plot of land with spare bedrooms, private driveways and swimming pools, has overshadowed our environmentally friendly, community-spirited nature; the epitome of 1980s materialism. To hammer this point home, Spielberg has the skeletons of the desecrated force their way into the house through the floor of the kitchen (the room previously shown as the centre of family interaction) and rise up out of the status-symbol

All images on these two pages
Poltergeist (MGM/BFI Stills)

swimming pool Diane has fallen into – literally tearing away at the foundations.

From the opening moments, we know that *Poltergeist* will end happily; Spielberg's signature will see to that. We know that this family's strength is their unifying love for each other. However, in 1975's *Amityville Horror* (Stuart Rosenberg) the family is depicted as splintered; the resident evil in the seemingly idyllic house can find an easy pressure point to gnaw at. The Lutz family have moved from the city to small-town America, embarking on a familiar transition for characters in horror movies: the dream of the perfect country house shattered by strange otherworldly forces. The local community is seemingly suspicious, eccentric, even backward, compared to the sophisticates of the city. This immediately enforces a sense of solitude and prevents any good neighbour relations developing. The house may be in disrepair but it is all a charming adventure for the young couple asserting their newfound home-owner status. But George Lutz is not the father of Kathy's children, who are struggling to call him

occupant looking through the banisters or perched at the top of the stairs.

Perhaps the device of an old, cold, empty house works so well in horror films because it contrasts with childhood images of lively, warm, family havens – supposedly representing the norm. A house stripped bare of furnishings, with visible wear and tear as evidence of faceless previous occupants, jars with these preconceived notions and conveys an unnerving sense of redundancy. An old house laid bare also implies a forcibly removed history; there is an inherent unease in the thought of what may have been removed. In horror films, this gives a house an immediate character, enabling it to come alive as one of the central players in the film's action. To begin to take root in a house, new residents will attempt to erase all traces of its human history. We need to feel safe and secure; to stamp our seal on a house until it becomes an extension of our own characters – only then does it become our home.

The idea of the house's history coming back to reclaim its space, and asserting its own character, plays on these insecurities. In *Poltergeist,* the history of the house is, until the climax, completely hidden underneath plush Modernism. However, in *Amityville*

The architecture of the house implies something ominous and foreboding

'Dad'. George and Kathy are anxious, almost desperate, to make this work and they have invested all their savings in their dream house.

Early on in the film, the viewer is made aware of supernatural forces at work when the real estate agent flees from the empty house, threatened by a cold draught. The house's history is revealed straight away in the storytelling process, and George and Kathy are fully aware that the son of the family who used to live there murdered his parents, brothers and sisters as they slept in their beds. As the estate agent shows them around each empty room, there is a quick cutaway to the son treading the same footsteps and shooting each member of his family in turn a year earlier. But as George says, 'Houses don't have memories'. However, the very architecture of the house implies something ominous and foreboding. This is achieved mainly through a well-chosen eerie soundtrack and carefully considered camera angles; scenes are shot as if from the viewpoint of another, unseen,

Horror, it is still resonant in the worn and stained architecture and every shot of the exterior is chilling. The idea of character is enhanced by the two attic windows in the arch of the roof, either side of the chimney breast and above balcony banisters that run the length of the exterior wall over the ground floor windows, giving the illusion of eyes, nose, teeth and hair. Later on in the film, we learn that this house, too, was built on an ancient, desecrated burial ground, its history of evil reaching back far earlier than its last occupants.

Near the conclusion of the film, George looks up at the house. A storm rages. The Lutzes are falling apart; they are broke, George is alienated from the children and he has become unpredictable and violent towards Kathy. The fragile nature of their new marriage has been strained. It is at this moment that George seems to realise that the house is to blame; it has somehow manipulated the family into arguments and fights through 'accidents' (windows slamming down on hands, doors locking babysitters into closets, etc). When George sees a devilish figure through the attic

Opposite top
Amityville Horror
(Castle Communications/
The Ronald Grant Archive)

Opposite bottom
Poltergeist (MGM/BFI Stills)

38

windows, he wields his axe and prepares to do battle with the house.

Whereas the house in *Poltergeist* wanted to be rid of the Freelings, in *Amityville Horror* it wants to hold the Lutzes prisoner. We learn that George's strange behaviour echoes that of the disturbed son of the previous family who lived there, as if he is gearing up to re-enact the terrible events of their last night. This is the house's final trick in using the Lutzes to practise its evil. When Kathy sees the axe-wielding George approaching the house, she is convinced he is coming to kill her and her children. She hides the kids and tries to wrestle the axe from him. In anticipation of the climactic battle of the warring Lutzes, the house begins to ooze blood from the walls, as if salivating with delight. But George is trying to save his family from the beast he saw through the attic window eyes. In a climax similar to that of *Poltergeist*, the Lutzes are reunited and together they find the determination to flee the house. They descend the bloodsoaked stairs and battle with the jammed front door, all the while glancing behind them as if something tangible is giving chase. This tense sequence is intercut with shots of the exterior 'face' of the house, lit up with flashes of lightning, as if the storm is expressing its anger. Lights shine through the attic windows enhancing the effect of angry eyes. The Lutzes finally escape. The last shot of the film is given to the face of the house, still intact, as if it has lost the battle but not the war.

Where *Poltergeist* and *Amityville Horror* deal with an ancient evil haunting a house trespassing in its space, Clive Barker's *Hellraiser* of 1987 deals with a new evil occupying an old house. Frank Cotton is squatting in his vacant family home before his brother Larry and new wife Julia arrive to take over occupancy. Whilst there, Frank summons the Cenobites – sadomasochistic travellers from Hell seeking living flesh to tease and torture. They literally tear Frank's body apart in their limitless quest for the ultimate pleasure. Although they apparently leave no physical traces, something of their visit remains, as if soaked into the architecture. The house becomes run-down, rat and maggot infested, and tacky religious paraphernalia adorns the dark, dank rooms. The visit from Frank and the Cenobites has subverted any warmth to a cold creepiness.

In a trick pioneered by Hammer's *Dracula*, when Larry's blood is accidentally spilt on the floorboards during removals, Frank starts to grow again: the floorboards absorb the blood and a heartbeat is heard, recalling Edgar Allen Poe's 'The Tell-Tale Heart'. The house acts as a vessel, incubating the formless Frank until he can become flesh again. The womblike qualities of the gap between ceiling and floorboard enable the new Frank to be born. First a beating heart, then limbs and torso sprout from an amniotic like fluid that oozes up and spreads across the floor where Frank was previously tortured and killed. He is soon walking and talking again, but without nerves and skin. Half the house is still undecorated and unfurnished by Larry and Julia and remains cold and dark. It is this half that Frank occupies, repelled by the warmth and normality of the occupied part, where the couple interact and entertain guests. The shadows of the house provide him with the protection he needs before he gets his skin back.

Barker uses the house like a cosseting mother to the two brothers, 'giving birth' to one and providing both with apparent safety and security in the familiar territory of their family home, responding to their different needs. Julia is caught between the two worlds in the house. Memories of a torrid affair with Frank before his death fuel her lust to be with him again – she accepts the horror of his situation and agrees to help him. But she is trapped in her loveless marriage with Larry, who repells her but provides her with security. During the film's climax, Julia and Frank conspire to kill Larry so that Frank can wear his skin. But Frank sacrifices Julia to ensure his own safety, revealing his purely selfish motivation and Julia's blind lust. This story is again based around a dysfunctional family, acting out their corrupt, deceptive relationships

– perhaps glossed over in *Poltergeist*, used well in *Amityville Horror*, but fully explored and indulged here, where the manifestation of evil that is unleashed in the house serves to illustrate the underlying, dark motivations of the protagonists' behaviour.

Larry's daughter from a previous marriage – Kirsty – is the one flawless character who, from the beginning, knows that Julia cannot be trusted. She is instinctively reluctant to stay in the house, sensing its negative atmosphere. It is Kirsty who accidentally discovers the existence of the Cenobites and is shown that Hell is just on the other side of the wall, waiting to force a pathway through into her home. Barker signifies the close proximity of Hell by shining blinding lights through cracks in the wall and the lines of mortar between the bricks – showing their flimsy, transgressable nature – before effortlessly opening up man-sized floor-to-ceiling gaps in the walls. Kirsty succeeds in fighting off the predatory Frank and Julia but is unable to save her foolish, easily deceived father.

However, she manages to send the Cenobites back to Hell and seal up the invasive gateways in the house; it is now empty again but whole and secure, putting to rest her family's troubles.

Another film from a Clive Barker story, 1992's *Candyman* directed by Bernard Rose, explores further the idea of domestic architecture causing evil to be unleashed. Here, it is the style of architecture that encourages the horror: a high-rise estate in a run-down part of Chicago, which has become a ghetto for the underprivileged black community. In another play on childhood nightmares constructed around the house, the residents of Cabrini Green – in the face of a series of unprovoked and undiscriminating murders – have adopted the urban myth of the Candyman. This mythical character, wronged in a previous life, will appear in search of new, innocent blood if you say his name five times in front of the mirror. As opposed to one family's nightmare, the entire community attributes the daily horror of their lives to this nightmarish evil. Cabrini Green is a desolate blot on an affluent metropolis;

strewn litter, dead trees and broken fences punctuate the grounds between the high-rises, which themselves are daubed with angry graffiti by the gangs of loitering teenagers who act as sentries in the doorways and stairwells, intimidating strangers. The residents are largely unseen, barricaded in with boarded-up windows and reinforced doors. We see the burnt-out shell of the last murder victim's apartment, decorated with graffiti and painted images of the Candyman that tell his story in an urban, streetwise discourse, perpetuating belief in his existence. Here, the gruesome history of the estate is bought to the fore. All remnants of human occupation are completely erased; the apartment has become a warning and a shrine.

The follies of quick-fix architecture and corrupt town planning are revealed to be the cause of the ghettoisation of the black community. The same high-rise architecture

to make sense of their enforced situation through fantasy. They are already victims of the racist system: their rich, white counterparts live in identical accommodation across town, but in apparent safety and comfort.

Early on in the film, we are made aware of Helen's troubled relationship with her husband. Trevor Lyle has a seat at the university, he gazumps her paper with his own lecture on the subject of urban myths and is also conducting an affair with one of his infatuated students. After they split, Helen returns, uninvited, to her marital home to find Trevor and his new lover redecorating; removing all evidence of their shared history. When the demoralised Helen unwittingly summons the Candyman into her apartment through her bathroom mirror, he murders her only friend. The safety of the luxury apartment is destroyed as the Candyman finds an easy access point, making the superficial decor redundant and revealing the condos to be as vulnerable as the apartments in Cabrini Green – the rich, white resident's ultimate paranoia. Helen's

The architecture has provided the Candyman with easy prey: deprived, depressed residents… a failed example of Le Corbusier's ideal

has been used in the construction of two separate developments. One group of high-rises with plaster covering the breeze blocks has been sold as trendy condos in the affluent sector, whilst the other is used as cheap housing for the poor across town and has been left to rot. The central character, Helen Lyle, who is researching urban myths for a university paper, lives in the condo development and believes the answer to the Cabrini Green murders is that substandard building enables the perpetrator to enter apartments through adjoining bathrooms – the mirrors can easily be removed, uncovering a hole between the two apartments, as she discovers herself in her condo when investigating the scene of the last murder. This lends weight to the idea that the Candyman strikes through the bathroom mirror, and to the resident's fear that they hear him 'coming through the walls'. The victim's screams are audible to all through the uninsulated walls. The very nature of the architecture has provided the Candyman with easy prey: deprived, depressed residents living in overcrowded battery cages – a failed example of Le Corbusier's ideal – and seeking

enforced solitude seemingly gives her no choice but to be brought under the Candyman's spell. She finds herself caught in his world; living in the spaces behind the bathroom mirrors in the high-rise apartments; feeding on the fear of those who believe in the myth; occupying the uninhabitable, deserted hovels of the Candyman's former victims until she herself becomes part of the myth.

Whilst trapping the Candyman in order to kill him, Helen sacrifices her own life. Her sad portrait becomes integrated into the storytelling graffiti on the walls of Cabrini Green, as she too becomes part of the estate's history, threatening to rise again to wreak revenge for her wrongful death, to perpetuate the Candyman myth, even in the luxury apartments. This, as she effectively does in the final scene when she slays the treacherous Trevor in their bathroom whilst his lover cooks for him in the kitchen.

Horror films like these are often reflections of our hidden, personal insecurities about families and relationships, where the house develops a character in order to become a representational protagonist. Whether you read them as childish fantasies or metaphors on modern living, one message predominates: we can never be completely safe from our imaginations in our homes. ⌂

Mall Movies

Rescue Strategie[s] and 'Bad' Architecture

Shopping malls have featured in films for over two decades. Stephanie Ellis discusses how women of colour, traditionally portrayed as excluded and repressed subjects in need of rescue, are placed within the suburban and downtown context of the American mall, and how its invisible, template architecture is subsequently engendered and racialised. She makes particular reference to Aretha Franklin in *The Blues Brothers* and Pam Grier in *Jackie Brown*.

Shopping malls have been featured in films for over 20 years. *Jackie Brown* (1997), *Clueless* and *Mallrats* (1995) and *True Stories* (1986) are recent examples. *Dawn of the Dead* (1979), *Blues Brothers* (1980) and *Fast Times at Ridgemont High* (1982), were among the first. Early mall films followed the peak of these suburban buildings in the 1970s. By that time, mall construction was a science. Planners calculated the choice of anchor stores, parking-lot size, the number and placement of entrances and the length of corridors to match a targeted community and maximise sales per square foot. Malls were a predictable and therefore appealing investment for pension and insurance funds. The repetition of successful mall formulas meant that those in similar communities were nearly identical. In addition, constant makeovers at successful malls produced a uniform freshness. Unlike 'high' architecture, whose value increases over time precisely because of an aura of history, malls must seem new or they aren't doing their job.

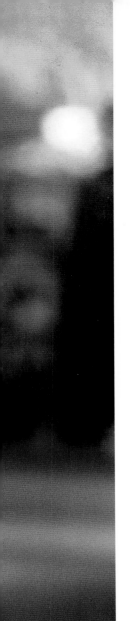

Malls appear self-evident: they look alike and have no history, so what's to say? It comes as no surprise that when film critics talk about malls they seldom describe the architecture in question. Dismissed as non-architecture, malls prop up the mystique of 'real' architecture as that which is motivated by something more generous than the bottom line. Often the humour, or even the plot, of these mall films spins around whether or not this 'bad' architecture has an unhealthy effect on its denizens. For the most part, the films describe a world of less than ideal citizens: girls of all ages, zombies, deadbeats, teenagers and Californians. Yet in the feminised terrain of the banal, the everyday, insignificant and mindless is celebrated as often as it is maligned. For instance, the notion that malls are non- or bad architecture can flip – they can become an anti-architecture. If the dystopic nature of malls and the ambiguity about their cultural influence now seems obvious, it is because the utopic moment of mall architecture is usually repressed.

At the 1939 New York World's Fair a film, *The City*, commissioned by the American Institute of City Planners, was shown for the first time. It opens with images of dirty, anxious children playing in the gutters of urban streets, followed by scenes of healthier, happier children riding bikes through a small grassy park nestled between low-key public buildings. The narrator tells the viewers that this city of tomorrow is 'here ... ready to serve a better age ... the choice is yours'. This Modernist rescue mission (the right architecture will build the right citizens) would reappear in the years after the Second World War, but with two differences: the world of tomorrow would not be in the city, and the specific address would not be to all citizens but to female consumers. Large government housing projects for returning GIs, built on tracts of cheap land isolated from existing retail areas, opened up an opportunity for the construction of a safe and relaxed retail environment conducive to transforming the chore of shopping into a leisure activity. This new version of a bright future was advanced by a small but influential number of avant-garde architects in government posts.

From the beginning, this green dream was a screen for white flight. The promotional images of ideal suburbanites as white, backed by discrimination practices in housing, made it clear that this ideal in retail architecture was not going to rescue women of colour. The mall was racialised at the same moment that it was feminised. In mainstream media stories about malls the exclusion of the woman of colour has never been a topic. Instead, racial and gender tensions embedded in mall architecture are displaced onto a narrative that is ostensibly about the health of the American city – a myth of municipal sickness and recovery that incidentally features the mall. The story has two parts. In the 1960s, suburban malls were known as the nightmare of downtown boosters. Malls were the 'new city' that happened not in the city but elsewhere, in the suburbs, leaving the decrepit downtown to continue its downward slide. Then, in the late 1970s, a new ideal middle-class residence – the urban loft – gained a glamour that put the suburban ranch house in the shade. Suburban homes became more loftlike: skylights, high ceilings and large open spaces. Downtown became more suburban as industrial zones were broken up by residential conversions and 'village' amenities such as small parks for dogs and children and family-friendly shopping, eating and entertainment. By the 1990s, under the new rubric of Urban Entertainment Destinations (UEDs), the myth was reversed. Malls became star players for upscale downtowns, competing against each other for corporate headquarters and tourists. In both narratives – the dying city/the rising city – malls are the architecture of the makeover, with the power to destroy or animate the urban core. The ability of malls constantly to update themselves, the trait that made this architecture 'bad' in the first place, is precisely the quality that makes them so pivotal in these stories of the city. Yet, despite this central role, the tensions of race and gender found in stories about the collapse and restoration of the city (which is also the story of how to locate whiteness and the American family), are absent from media coverage of mall architecture. It is only at the level of everyday conversation and geographies that these tensions reappear. Signs of decay translate as signs of colour. Despite the UEDs appeal to multicultural professionals, the appearance of these safe playgrounds for the cosmopolitan class has not changed the truism that an old mall is an ethnic mall – a cliché since the production of malls peaked in the 1970s.

The Hollywood films *The Blues Brothers* and *Jackie Brown* are haunted by the historically excluded figure of the woman of colour. Both films ask whether she is the subject or author of a rescue scenario. In each case, the ambivalence is mediated by the camera's relationship to panoramic spectatorship. By panoramic spectatorship, I mean both a panoramic object – landscapes, seascapes and cityscapes, and the implied panoramic subject, who has an unimpeded gaze at the centre of a vast horizon – what the artist Allan Sekula has called a 'vision of greed'. The ideal panoramic vista is one of mastery. In contemporary cityscapes, it is the high architecture of the financial district that

conventionally stands in for the entire city. In each of these mall movies, the strategic point of view presumed by this iconic urban image is unsettled by the tactics of a woman of colour.

For the writer Michel de Certeau, making everyday practices an object of study allows for an understanding of how the intent of a power structure is constantly misinterpreted or mistranslated. He offers a rough dichotomy between strategies and tactics. Those with a power base have strategies: long-range and widely implemented social plans. Those without a power base (the subjects rather than the authors of strategies) have tactics: short-term and impromptu tricks to achieve a desired end. *The Blues Brothers* ostensibly recounts a series of tactics by two disenfranchised brothers on 'a mission from God' to save an inner-city Catholic orphanage from eviction. The two small-time Chicago hoods, Jake and Elwood, promise the mother superior that they will pay its taxes without resorting to crime. Their plan is to reassemble their blues band for a sell-out gig. The humour of the film relies on the unlikely proposition that these two reprobates who profess to have black music in their souls are entitled to an unchallenged panoramic vision.

The film opens with a panorama of Chicago. This vast, sentimental skyline sets up the Blues Brothers' task as a mission from God: the unimpeded vision from on high. Furthermore, Jake is twice bathed in light, indicating that his range of vision exceeds the ordinary. The pair's trademark dark glasses serve as a code for this superior sight. Finally, Jake and Elwood's adventures culminate in a classic of urban mobility, the successful climb – defying the city police, state troopers, federal troops, Nazis and rednecks who try to stop them – to the top of a skyscraper. They own the big picture. They also act as if they own their own mall. In some ways, they do.

In the documentary, *'The Making of The Blues Brothers'*, John Landis bragged that *The Blues Brothers* is 'the first film to trash a mall'. Viewers saw storefront after storefront shatter as the Bluesmobile and cop cars careered down one side of the mall and up another. Given the film's concessions to a contemporary backlash against feminism, setting up boys with toys against shoppers was perhaps not so novel. What is interesting is that these shots, which were produced prior to computerised special effects, required the unearthing and resuscitating of an abandoned mall that was subsequently destroyed.

Furthermore, the maze of the mall provides four minutes of continuous smashing. The tally of destruction on screen and in production received wide press. The marketing strategy was of panoramic logic, based on the hope that having the biggest, the longest, and the most makes a picture that sells the most for the longest.

Given the infamous legacy of Chicago protests and riots, an emerging environmental conservation movement and an enormous youth market, *The Blues Brothers* played its excesses ironically, thus providing a foil for the film's heart of gold. On screen, two white men in black save orphans. In the production promos, two white men and a white director save the blues. In the production documentary that accompanies the video release, John Landis claims, 'You talk to James Brown or Aretha Franklin or any of these people and they'll tell you that their careers were revitalised. I'm proud of that'. The rescue of Aretha Franklin's career was a major press story. When the film's exploitation of big scores did not produce the expected box office, some critics countered that it was Aretha Franklin, in fact, who rescued the film. In the movie, she sings a song called 'Think'. The refrain is: 'I need you and you need me, without each other there ain't nothing neither can do.' If the reviewers had written in black vernacular, they might have said that without Aretha there ain't nothing for nobody to see. In the architecture of black grammar, negatives don't cancel each other out; instead they enjoy a certain mobility, reiterating and building on the same sentiment from several positions within the sentence. Unlike Landis, whose rescue narrative is framed by an either/or split between the author and the subject of a rescue narrative, Aretha Franklin offers a scenario of co-production.

'Characters live in spacious worlds and know a lot of people (in most thrillers the characters know only each other). The sides

Above left and right
The Blues Brothers
(Universal/BFI Stills)

Opposite
Jackie Brown
(Photo: Darren Michaels, courtesy Miramax)

44

of the film's canvas are free to expand when it is necessary.'
—Roger Ebert, *Chicago Sun-Times* review of *Jackie Brown*.

'Jackie Brown... [is] going to survive all those people ... making decisions for her – which is what I have had to do. It was like a building hit me, and I was able to crawl out from underneath and walk away.'
—Pam Grier interviewed in *Entertainment Weekly on-line*.

Almost 20 years after *The Blues Brothers*, Quentin Tarantino's *Jackie Brown* repeats many of the same motifs – single-minded cops, black music, a long sequence in a mall, nostalgic rescues. This time, however, the central protagonist is a woman of colour. Some critics felt the film lacked the action and violence they admired in Tarantino's other films. One writer found it sluggish, with everyday 'anecdotes told at epic length'. Tarantino was accused of playing 'peekaboo with his sizeable talent'. On the other hand, what critics who liked the film, like Ebert, admired was precisely this constant scratching for space, the delight of tactics. If the embrace of the panoramic in *The Blues Brothers* undercuts as much as it establishes the protagonists' claim to being hip pranksters, the refusal of the panoramic by Tarantino brilliantly secures Jackie Brown as the ultimate trickster.

The opening scene in the film is a frustrated panorama. Jackie Brown is a flight attendant who has a sideline smuggling illegal gun money out of Mexico. Tarantino could easily have opened with a deep shot from the plane window or an image of the plane flying over Los Angeles. Instead, a profile of Jackie Brown, played by Pam Grier, fills the screen. What appears at first to be a mug shot is in fact Brown in flight uniform striding across a moving airport walkway. This parody of a cinematic pan refuses access to anything else – figures, windows, potted plants, pictures or posters. There is only the woman of colour's stone profile and an endless blue tile wall.

This refusal of the panoramic is maintained throughout the film, but is most definitive in the scenes at the Del Amo Mall. The money exchange in the mall is seen three times, each time from the viewpoint of a different protagonist. Jackie, caught between the feds and a gun dealer, must convince the feds that the money she is delivering to her boss was unexpectedly stolen from her when, in fact, she

has passed the money to her partner. She relies on the feds' underestimation of her intelligence to convince them that she was seduced into shopping, thus blowing their entrapment gig. She runs through the mall, looking wildly from side to side. The camera spins around her as she turns and turns, calling the lawmen from their cover. Her tactic is the performance of vertigo, a negative position in panoramic spectatorship – when the vastness of the big picture impacts the subjects at the centre to such an extent that they feel small and overwhelmed, losing rather than gaining mastery. Jackie's feigning of vertigo in the mall is convincing because it fulfils the feds' miscalculation of an older black woman's courage and ambition. On the other hand, the vertigo of Louis, the gun dealer's sloppy sidekick who unravels before the endless horizon of the mall parking lot and shoots his boss' mistress, is unimaginable to the feds, who make yet another wrong reckoning. To both the law and the outlaw, Jackie Brown appears to co-operate. Only the viewer and the white bondsman are privy to her moves on her own behalf. Her tactics drive the film; even the bondsman who helps her is animated by her, not the reverse.

On screen, she is far from the subject of rescue. Off screen, the story is more complicated. In the promotions surrounding the release of the film, Tarantino was lauded for rescuing Pam Grier's career from the 'twilight' that followed her fame as blaxploitation queen the 1970s. Echoing the claims that Landis made about Aretha Franklin. Tarantino takes credit for this while clearly banking on Grier as a nostalgic figure. Some reviewers suggest that, in fact, it was Grier who saved Tarantino from a career stall. Always respectful of Tarantino, when Grier is asked about the recent attention she is receiving she chooses to tie the revival of her career to the success of rap and hip-hop that rekindled an interest in 1970s black aesthetics. The feds tell Jackie Brown, 'You're 44 years of age flying for the shittiest little shuttle fucking shit piece of Mexican airlines there is'. The threat is clear: Jackie Brown has 'little room' to manoeuvre. She herself acknowledges that position: 'If I lose this job ... I'll be stuck with whatever I can get.' Yet, even after accepting that she is cornered, Jackie Brown successfully exploits her limited space, in this case the very architecture of the mall, against itself and to her own advantage.

Pam Grier indentifies with Jackie Brown's ability to get out of tight places. She and Jackie can survive falling buildings and walk away. For Grier, black aesthetics has a life of its own – in fact, many lives, since animation is a process rather than a given. In her story, as in Aretha Franklin's song, the 'bad' – ie unsafe – architecture of rescue is ditched for a fabric of co-production. ◿◹

Footnotes
1. *The Practice of Everyday Life*, Michel de Certeau, University of California Press (Berkeley), 1984.
2. *The New York Times*, Janet Maslin, June 20, 1980.
3. *Time*, 'Jackie Brown', Richard Corliss, December 22, 1997.
4. *Time*, 'Back in Action', Jeffrey Resner, August 18, 1997
5. *Jet*, Pam Grier interview, April 13, 1998.

Articulating the Cinematic Urban Experience in the City of Make-believe

In the late 20th century, cinematic film has developed as the most 'urban art' and Los Angeles as one of the most constant of celluloid backdrops. Martin Price explores dystopian and utopian images of LA, as seen in particular in Michael Mann's *Heat* and in the recent series of '*Hood*' films, in pursuit of the truer and more pragmatic portrayal of the metropolis.

Seen from the vantage point of the late 20th century, the global cities of the northern and southern hemispheres struggle to adapt to changing patterns and rhythms in all areas of social, economic, political and cultural life. The culture of cities, in fact, currently provides the dynamic at the centre of much contemporary cultural theory and debate.

Nowhere are the discourses relating to time, space and identity in the city demonstrated more powerfully and effectively than in their relationship to the cinema. But, as David Clarke has noted,

> despite the immediately perceptible cinematic qualities that cities frequently seem to possess, and despite the uncredited role played by the city in so many films, relatively little theoretical attention has been directed towards understanding the relationship between urban and cinematic space. Indeed, whilst the histories of film and the city are imbricated to such an extent that it is unthinkable

that the cinema would have developed without the city, and while the city has been unmistakenly shaped by the cinematic form, neither film nor urban studies has paid the warranted attention to their connection.[1]

Cinema has long had a close and many-sided relationship with the metropolitan city, investigating its strengths and its weaknesses. Generations of writers have argued that film itself evolved as an 'urban art', frequently articulating its narratives against the backdrop of the metropolitan city. Drawing upon the theoretical insights of Benjamin, Baudrillard and Foucault, my intention is to demonstrate that cities have grown increasingly complex, to the point where it is no longer viable to see them in simple axioms. To see the city as either entirely a utopia or dystopia is no longer a satisfactory consensual framework for analysis, if indeed, it ever really was.

Empirical realities have fused with urban mythologies, blurring the boundaries around the city and its cinematic representations. Benjamin tells us that what he set out to do was to devise an innovative, appropriate mode of representation for the city, examining the complex relationships between the organisation of time, space and human activity in the urban environment. Relying on Benjamin and others as guides, the focus of this essay will revolve around the city of Los Angeles and some of its cinematic representations.

The city for Benjamin was magnetic: it attracted and repelled him in the same moment. Although it was beautiful, beloved, congenial and vital for his literary production, Benjamin was never fully convinced that the urban complex could be the site of lasting contentment. It is this paradox, this unresolved tension, that lies at the heart of our own, as well as Benjamin's, fascination with the modern metropolis. Its architecture, spaces, street life, inhabitants and daily routines are a recurring set of themes in Benjamin's oeuvre. Indeed, his writings on the city are concerned with critically unmasking the delusions, pretensions and barbarism of that urban environment and social milieu that he found so indispensable. Urban life was essential to Benjamin, yet also barely tolerable. He both loved and loathed the city.

Cultural theorists Frederic Jameson and Umberto Eco have called LA the capital of 'Postmodernity', the hyperspace of a new social ontology; and as Mike Davis points out, if one of its co-ordinates is its exceptionalism, the other is its conceit that it is the future. One of the great American cities, it is both the most intimately familiar and the least known. It has plenty of rhetoric but no evident epistemology. Its imagery is everywhere, accumulating in our TV sets like unwanted daydreams. Only recently, LA has come to be seen as the exemplar of urban restructuring. Throughout the last decade, its greater metropolitan area has undergone economic, social, political and cultural upheavals deeper and broader than those experienced by any other large American city during the same period. In other words, 'within the galaxy of the US city system, Los Angeles is the supernova that lights the contemporary sky'.[2]

Contemporary cinema polarises our conceptions of the urban environment

In the film *Heat* (1995), Michael Mann creates a virtual city of attraction and repulsion. He reinvents LA with the same visual gaze he turned on Miami in the TV series *Miami Vice*, Las Vegas in *Crime Story* and Atlanta in *Manhunter* (1986). The exquisite attention to *mise en scene*, the careful framing of public buildings, public space and the architecture of downtown; his choice of colour and ability to paint with light, all testify to his extraordinary filmcraft. The amalgamation of these skills conspires to present us, the audience, with the most emotionally and aesthetically compelling arrangement of images. Like Benjamin, we are attracted and repelled in the same moment, for as Mann is seducing us with Postmodern representations in colour, texture and surface detail, he inculcates us into the violent psychotrauma of life in contemporary LA. Both Benjamin and Mann realise that the urban complex is the social totality that encapsulates the characteristic features of modern and Postmodern social and economic structures.

The imageries of the city are built on the shifting idioms of time, space and identity, projecting a multidimensional picture of urban life. The character of the city may be read from its numerous faces as Benjamin notes: 'In thousands of eyes, in thousands of objects, the city is reflected.'[3]

An extremely diverse stream of analysis on the contemporary experience of urban life has emerged from a disparate assortment of critics, novelists, philosophers and social theorist (Mike Davis, William Gibson, Frederic Jameson, Manuel Castells, Paul Virilio and David Harvey). Far from unified, they all nevertheless share similar perspectives focusing on the dystopian tendencies in the processes alleged to be under way – usually in North American cities –

towards more polarised, fragmented and divided places. The rapidly evolving sites for the expansion of communications technologies are alleged to put cities into increasingly vulnerable situations, often at the mercy of globally operating corporate economic power; to trap them in a vortex and violent spiral of decay, poverty and polarisation; and to underpin the packaging of urban landscapes into commodified fragments that are tightly controlled to maximise consumption. For Davis, the reality of contemporary Los Angeles already goes beyond what he calls the caricature of Ridley Scott's *Blade Runner* (1982). Rather, he builds on William Gibson's science fiction to map out the highly polarised and militarised urban-present of LA, where advanced communication technologies underpin the social segmentations – the surveillance and control – and maintenance of spatial power within the fragmented metropolis.

heterotopia. The heterotopia is capable of juxtaposing in a single real place several spaces that are in themselves incompatible. He is asserting that a classic or traditional concern with history and temporality persists across Modernism until around the end of the 1960s. These observations become retrospectively significant. The epoch that he envisaged, in which the transformation of space looks forwards to transformations beyond Modernism, we have since learned to name, live with and live into. From the heart of the Modernist 1960s, an as yet unnamed theme announces itself: Postmodernism. It is this shifting in the terrain, the sense of spatialisation, or rather the relationship between temporality and spatialisation that we might read in a variety of texts as solidly pre-postmodern. Images of the city in this Foucaultian sense reveal it as both utopia and dystopia, presenting itself as primary metaphor for the late 20th-century Postmodern urban experience.

Los Angeles is often cited as the symbol of Postmodern urban problems. A city at once endlessly

LA is at once endlessly familiar to us through its representation in television and cinematic images and yet endlessly strange and distant

Here, the primary layers of the urban nightmare are articulated – the dark, unstoppable technological and economic forces at work encouraging a greater social polarisation and alienation within cities. The fractured and ambiguous site that is the current Los Angeles is an amorphous polysemic amalgamation of cultural enclaves where dystopian visions and utopian ideals coalesce in stormy matrimony. Reyner Banham considers LA not so much a utopia as an autopia, acknowledging that 'the freeway system in LA in its totality is now a single comprehensible place, a coherent state of mind, a complete way of life, the fourth ecology of the 'Angeleno'.

It was Michel Foucault who encouraged us to think of the two moral dimensions of the city as present simultaneously in the same physical space. A lecture he delivered in 1967 anticipates something of the themes explored in the cinematic city. Foucault speculated that Western culture was undergoing a change in experience of the structuring of time and space and their relation. He theorised the possibility of the

familiar to us through its representation in television and cinematic images and yet infinitely strange and distant.

Paula Massood's work in *Mapping the Hood* explores this utopian/dystopian dialectic from the point of view of urban Afro-American experiences and perspectives to reveal the complexities of space and temporality. Films such as *Boyz N the Hood*, *Straight Out of Brooklyn*, *Juice*, *Menace II Society*, and *Just Another Girl on the IRT* share a number of technical similarities. They all:

detail the hardships of coming of age for their young protagonists and all locate their narratives within the specific geographic boundaries of the Hood. Within this context, the Hood inhabits precise co-ordinates: South Central LA, Watts, Brooklyn and Harlem. At the same time, it also encompasses a range of possible metaphorical meanings as an urbanscape, meanings which extend beyond the domain of the contemporary hood-film genre and are informed by a rich history of African American urban representation.[4]

The cityscape of the *Hood* film is largely determined by, and firmly entrenched in, this multilayered historical and cultural legacy, a legacy in which the city has been mythologised as both a utopia – as a space promising freedom and economic mobility – and a dystopia – the ghetto's economic impoverishment and segregation. In this manner, the city as a signifying space has performed a dual function, both real and imaginary. This duality is one which has been explained as an ongoing dialogue, a dialogue that sets a city of the imagination, the city that one wants, against the empirical reality of the city one has. Hood films, firmly placed within this tradition, self-consciously examine this duality by making complex their representation of the cityscape.[5]

Few cities are as well equipped for an exploration of the tension between the real and the imaginary of city signification as LA, 'a city that was founded upon and has prospered because of the manufacture of reality through the imaginary, both in its

are capable of development but which are now frozen in dream images.

Attempting to understand how urban space is used in the context of the metropolitan city and its subsequent representations in the cinema requires seeing the city with double vision. In *Heat,* Mann forces us to view urban space as double-textured. To understand the complexities of the labyrinthine city requires Modernist as well as Postmodernist visions.

The city, as James Donald views it, 'is better understood as a historically specific mode of seeing, a structure of visibility that incorporates not only the analytic epistemology theorised by Benjamin'[7] but also the visual sorties in imagination hypothesised and realised in the fantastic cities of Hollywood.

This structure of visibility is, as I see it, a multilayered, multitextured mode of seeing that penetrates the social and economic, as well as the time and spatial configurations in urban and cinematic discourse. The early 20th century city explored by Benjamin, Sergei Eisenstein, Charlie Chaplin,

Los Angeles broadcasts its self-imagery so widely that probably more people have seen this place than any other place on the planet

Footnotes
1. *The Cinematic City,* Introduction: 'Previewing the Cinematic City', David Clarke, Routledge, (London), 1997, pp 1–14.
2. *Homeowners and Homeboys: Urban Restructuring in LA,* Mike Davis, Enclictic/Summer, 1989, pp 9–10.
3. *Myth and Metropolis: Walter Benjamin and the City,* Graeme Gilloch, Polity Press, 1996, pp 1–7.
4. *Mapping the Hood: The Genealogy of City Space in Boys N the Hood and Menace II Society,* Paula J Masood, *Cinemas Journal* 35, no 2, 1996, pp 85–90.
5. Ibid.
6. Ibid.
7. *Imagining Cities: Scripts, Signs, Memory,* Sallie Westwood and John Williams (eds), Routledge, (London), 1997, p 181.

particular self-image and those images produced in Hollywood'.[6]

As Edward Soja has said, 'Los Angeles broadcasts its self-imagery so widely that probably more people have seen this place – or at least fragments of it – than any other place on the planet'.

It is through the processes of inclusion and exclusion that Hollywood has helped LA to nurture and reify a particular set of urban signifiers – palm trees, sun, abundance, paradise. Yet the manufacture of one particular group of images has as its mirror the exclusion of the areas that do not meet the criteria for this imagined city.

In *Heat,* Mann rejected the familiar earth tones, emphasising instead subdued pastels, cobalt and Pacific blues, titanium silver and fluorescent yellow. His use of lighting, camera angles, cutting and sound capture the high-tech multiracial culture of downtown. Mann's dystopic visualisation of LA is turned into aesthetic spectacle, conveying images that are violent, compelling and seductive.

Returning to Benjamin, modernity was a store of dialectical images bearing contradictions that

FW Murnau and Fritz Lang has undergone, if not radical transformation, then significant historical change. Late capitalism, or the arrival of Postmodernism, has ruptured the flow of rational philosophy and progress. As the city has expanded and developed, it has become increasingly difficult to sustain any stable ideological position. Even when one stops to consider the work of Baudrillard, the picture is far from clear. It is worth remembering that the 'Postmodern', in any event, may be considered a part of the 'modern', and many people are far from convinced of the marked conceptual shift from Modernity to Postmodernity that some critics find in the development of Baudrillard's work.

The city in the late 20th century is viewed through a sophisticated set of visual and analytic discourses that not only capture the 'trace elements' of its populations, but may also herald a new urban imagination, new structures of visibility, a new pragmatic aesthetic that transcends the conventional theories of urban space and more closely approximates the world of Foucault's heterotopia. Its contours are hinted at in the delirious utopia/dystopia architectural narratives of LA as well as in the spatial geometries of modern and postmodern cinema. Δ

49

LA

and the Architecture of Disaster

The sweeping and saturated freeways of Los Angeles provide
the wide-screen canvas on which the film-maker can effectively
orchestrate the cinematic spectacle of disaster. With David
Cronenberg's *Crash* and David Lynch's *Lost Highway*, Jonathan
Bell effectively illustrates how the collusion of architecture
and disaster provides a 'landscape of uncertainty' across
which crawls the mobile Mecca of the car.

Los Angeles, gracious host and frequent subject of American cinema, is rarely granted the courtesy of a 'straight' celluloid depiction. Instead, the city has become a blank canvas on which to depict the neuroses of city life. Los Angeles is a town founded on myth and legend, a sprawl of tales and stories stretching for 465 square miles that has inspired myth-makers and storytellers to weave threads of civic experience into their work, art mirroring their environment. The countless celluloid lies that have been born beneath the picture-perfect skies reflect a city of imitation, duplicity, simulation and duplication. As Reyner Banham noted in *The Architecture of Four Ecologies*,

> in 1910 the movie industry found Los Angeles a diffuse fruit-growing super-village of some eight hundred thousand souls and handed it over to the infant television industry in 1950 a world metropolis of over four million.[1]

A world metropolis best known for freeways, films, crime and crazies, an intertwined miasma of cultures and cars, LA is cinema, albeit cinema crawling along one of the world's largest freeway systems at an average speed of 17 mph.

LA is a vast cinematic playground, a showreel of possibilities whose horizontal quality lends itself to the format of the 35mm film camera. The tumultuous expansion, spurred by the railways, the fruit growers, the oil industry and finally by Tinseltown, has left only faint scars of transport and past routes. LA's lack of instant identity is advantageous in the language of film, where the anonymity at street level re-creates a thousand locations. The film industry grew rich on this arid, dusty plain, with vacant lots transformed through carpentry, cloth and paint into great vistas and historical landscapes. The low hills of Universal Studios contain the relics of a hundred urban dramas, their thin facades awaiting renewal for another brush with fame. The studios are lit by a free, billion-candlelight orb that stops only to set in an orgy of flaming colour, a cherry-red special effect that can be both apocalyptic and romantic.

In this land of rapid change and multifaceted identity, architecture soared and roared and screamed for attention. But the skyline could not compete with the horizon and the frontiersman's desire to shrink this ever-constant distance. Automotive culture compresses speed, time and scale and LA's verticality is merely illusory. Witness the orange globe of the '76 gas station

chain atop its slender pole; or Simon Rodia's Watts' Towers, testament to a lifetime's accumulation, casting Gaudiesque shadows on the tough, wiry lawns and gridded doors of the aluminum-sided neighbourhood below. For commentators like Banham, Venturi and Moore, the decorated shed – the building as sign – was the apotheosis of a cultural condition, a new form of urbanity. LA is a city of motion, seen from the car or through the screen. A bit-part player in a million scenes, the city is thronged with familiar faces, flicking past at 24 frames per second, conveyed by a lens that chooses to pervert, subvert or destroy in order to catch our attention.

The disaster is a key part of LA's cinematic image. In an age of road rage (the city's most successful export) rush hour is a time of simmering tensions, drifting from bumper to bumper, waiting to explode. Guidebooks hint darkly at road rage, car-jacking, drive-bys – violent episodes that have come to characterise the city through their exploitation and celebration in cinematic violence. In *Falling Down* (Joel Schumacher, 1993), Michael Douglas' character D-Fens becomes enraged as his vehicle sits in traffic, and subsequently wreaks revenge on an impersonal city bubbling with the friction from a hundred cultures. The film, in which the freeway acts as the catalyst for violence, was made as the real-life post-Rodney King riots of April 1992 erupted bloodily on the streets, killing 58 people.

The roads choke as well as inflame. The automobile pumps out pollutants, creating a dense cloud of fumes that hangs over the plain like a pall, filtering the sunset and soiling the complexion of this otherwise health-obsessed city. Smogs appeared as early as the 1940s, an appropriately neobiblical vengeance on a town that grew fat on the lavish interwar re-creations of mythical plague, pestilence and disaster for the delight of millions of cinemagoers. Cars continue to swarm like locusts, doubling to nine million between 1961 and 1979.[2] In 1978, the California Department of Transport declared that the freeways were saturated. Now, over two decades later, these sweeping 10-lane concrete curves remain, while the volume of traffic and pollution is on an ever upward spiral. The highways form a gigantic grid that will drive the city onwards, dominating all future debate on transport. By the late 1990s, the LA 2000 Committee was predicting that even after the completion of the Metro Rail project in 2001, 96 per cent of Angelenos would still travel by car, their personal space in an increasingly impersonal city.

Constantly assailed by natural cataclysm, and culturally predisposed towards epic levels of prophetic hyperbole, Los Angeles is synonymous with disaster, whether man-made, natural or imaginary. Mike Davis charts LA's progress through a century of travails in *Ecology of Fear*, revealing the cinematic self-abuse of a city of masochists. Sitting astride the twitchy San

Andreas fault, the city is permanently threatened with distillation into powdered concrete, speckled with the blood of the unfortunate, as the soaring elevated freeways snap tightly shut like a vast carnivorous plant devouring its prey. Throughout its history, LA has endured plagues, floods, bush fires, predators, droughts, mud slides and earthquakes, all lovingly catalogued in *Ecology of Fear*. Davis cites 138 novels and films since 1909 that have used the destruction of LA as a central theme, examples of the self-flagellating seeking self-fulfilment, a masochistic streak like a yawning chasm in the tired, unstable earth. Ultimately, even coating the landscape with a thick crust of tarmac and concrete has done little to tame the elements.

LA's distinctive signature is broken into a plethora of identities, a portmanteau of Day-Glo billboards and buildings, forming an architectural zoo worthy of a thousand college papers and countless academic treatises. Cinematically, LA lends itself well to these sun-drenched collages of exaggerated cliché – babes on rollerblades, glistening muscle-bound torsos, low-riding wide boys, the grim, mirror-faced LAPD, bag-laden Rodeo Drive divas – as they mill about the pastel-facaded burger joints, the neon strips fringed with palm trees, the air-conditioned malls, the schoolyards, the beaches. The emasculated 'Hollywoodland' sign on the horizon is our constant reminder of place, as if one were needed. LA in the movies is a city of people and signs; people as signs.

Has cinema ever attempted to portray contemporary LA as *noir*? Leaving aside the obvious futuristic dystopia of *Blade Runner*, or the postwar, Chandleresque of *LA Confidential*, contemporary films that play off the city's subtler aspects are scarce on the ground. Bright lights and loud noises signal LA, as mainstream film-makers relish the chance to wreak havoc on their home turf. *Beverly Hills Cop*, *Lethal Weapon*, *Die Hard*, *Bad Boys*, *Speed* and countless others, all ladle on the mayhem on, rather than draw it from within. Buildings are there to be destroyed, parked cars crushed, sidewalks mounted, meters snapped and the freeways ploughed up from end to end in glorious Technicolor. The city's trademark locations become synonymous with action in LA's celluloid image. The concrete riverbeds act as conduits for plot and motion, rather than as coherent expressions of the city's identity. The truck powering its way through the narrow concrete canyons in *Terminator 2* (James Cameron, 1991) was oblivious to its urban

surroundings. The apocalyptic visions of *Independence Day* (Roland Emmerich, 1996) delighted in throwing the city's nemesis, the car, aside like scrap paper, filleting buildings so that their windows streamed out in slender rivulets of glass. The future metropolis, a few hundred miles west of the nuclear test sites of the Nevada desert, can seemingly only inspire and invite destruction.

Jan de Bont's epic *Speed* flew in the face of traditional structure by eschewing format and presenting itself as one long climax; tantric film-making, peaking in ever-increasing crescendos. The film shows LA as linear city, shunning the initial drama of height and depth anticipated in the opening elevator sequence. *Speed*'s LA is an endless road threaded through anonymous urban scenery; a horizontal journey pegged at constant speed by psychopathic intervention through the city's constantly evolving hinterlands. Even a freeway leading into the void – an Angeleno nightmare realised in recent earthquakes – fails to halt the bus's progress. Act Two culminates in an airport, the horizontalist's apotheosis, the concrete fetishist's dream. LAX's open expanses of warm tarmac are ripe for the laying of burning rubber, glamorous pyrotechnics twisting and turning, spinning and endless. *Bad Boys* is also set in an LA of motion. Characters drive, cars are worshipped, confrontations occur across acres of road. Again, the climatic scene at an airport represents the orgiastic culmination of cinematic and automotive fantasies. The freeways are simultaneously southern California's 'grandest public artworks' and their greatest public liability. The off-ramp is a uniquely American symbol of death and disaster – celebrity murders, *The Bonfire of the Vanities*, the car jacker, *Clueless*, freeway hell, crushed to death by a Richterous tremor. This carefully calculated concrete curve, an unknown vector steering one against one's will at an unknown tangent, is to be exited at your peril as you are lured from the expressway into the unknown, away from the comforting rumble from seamlessly joined concrete slabs.

LA *noir* is an undernourished but persistent genre. Davids Lynch and Cronenberg, Wim Wenders and William Friedkin, amongst other directors, have avoided the easy path translating LA, or at least an approximation of LA, into a Hopperesque vision of razor-sharp shadows and *noirish* curves, using a muted palette of colours that belies the city's traditional image. Blacking out the sun, they imbue the metropolis with dark shadows and velvet colours, plunging its starry fingers into the inky darkness of the bordering desert as if this were the dark recess of the city's soul. The trailer trash, the auto-wrecking yard, the dusty, stifled derrick, black gold long since dried up, all figure in this environment of menace.

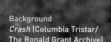

David Cronenberg's adaptation of JG Ballard's *Crash* transfers the book's claustrophobic location from London's Westway, with its orbital ring roads, grimy buildings, suffocating suburbs and the overhead throaty groan of airliners, to the sun-bleached 10-laners of the West Coast. Grit and claustrophobia give way to glacial, passionless erotica in glassy modern apartments. The freeway dominates the frame, a sinuous kinetic sculpture of traffic, the 'rivers of molten metal'.[3] Ballard and Catherine gaze down on this strangely muted sight from their balcony: the monumental concrete aprons, traffic gliding along like viscous liquid, golden engine oil, flowing between the rigorous symmetry of the apartment blocks – the sketchy proposals for the Ville Radieuse made flesh. In reality, Ontario doubled for LA, making *Crash* a curio, a cross-dressing sexual fantasy where nothing is what it seems. But this duplicity is persuasive; by ignoring the typical visual signifiers, LA is revealed as nothing more than a blank canvas, a yawning metropolis that can be re-created anywhere, anyhow. Globalised, big-city automotive culture makes location irrelevant. The grim, grimy, low-ceilinged sodium-lit multistorey car park, or the lofty undercrofts of cathedral-like elevated roadways, are anonymous and anytown. *Crash* is about destruction, the twisted, melded metal on the freeway deconstructing forms as Frank Gehry's Santa Monican house deconstructed the suburban box. The impacts and pile-ups are reduced in visceral intensity, the sheer size of the freeway system creates another form of claustrophobia, that of being trapped above the grid.

The freeway, with it's 'constant and unswerving geometry'[4] is disaster LA's principal celluloid symbol of architecture. LA is about travel, the distance between two places, a life in the car, the terror of the freeway, the terror off the freeway; a culture in love with the car, in love with death. The classic view of an America as observed by Jack Kerouac, Robert Frank, Hunter S Thompson and Ken Kesey, blinded to its problems by the desire to keep travelling, is reflected in LA cinema. Film exacerbates the dislocation of place through an emphasis on pace. We travel, through the camera and the characters, on endless, lost highways, the jarring impacts hurling us into the present. Of course, LA has character, architectural merit, a place in the textbooks, and it is no coincidence that the chroniclers of Postmodernism, Jameson,

Jencks and Soja, have looked to the city as a model for societal trends and directions. LA's sense of place is parlous, fragmentary, and key locations have their cinematic associations so culturally ingrained as to render them almost parodic to a contemporary audience. *Rebel Without a Cause*'s (Nicholas Ray, 1955) use of the LA Observatory, Frank Lloyd Wright's Ennis Brown House's endless list of cameos, the garish facades of Venice Beach and the steep hillsides buttressed by the gated driveways of the rich and famous are familiar the world over. All of these roles are valid, an association between architecture and film that mirrors the diversity of urban expansion.

In *Crash*, accidents are implicitly about vehicles interacting with each other rather than with inanimate objects, leaving the architecture of the built environment to be glossed over. Instead, highway engineering becomes the architecture, the solid mass of traffic becomes a great city, crawling along at rush-hour pace. *Crash*'s frigid characters are framed by frigid non-architecture, overpasses, bridges, the door pillar of a car, all tarnished and faded by the sun. The film's depiction of LA as a shapeless, directionless mass of traffic hardly refers to architecture at all, save in the Ballards' blank, sterile apartment. The few interiors depicted – hospitals, studios and car showrooms – all have an aura of unreality: either chaotic and busy film sets, or sterile, scrubbed environments. The freeways make their own gradients, with ramps, car parks and roadways creating a shifting terrain. Under these titanic concrete hulks lie the wrecks, the rusting hulks of crashed cars, relegated to life out of sight below the action, out of the sun. The emphasis is on the underside of the city – the multistorey car parks and the underpasses, the hidden spaces of cinematic enquiry. These concrete accretions seem as if whole cities had been razed to powder and flattened with a trowel, inscribed by the complex markings of a society dependent on autoculture. Cars are only fetishised once they are crumpled and inert, small architectural statements frozen in the last moment of their life. The camera lovingly lingers on the aftermath of collision, the Miesian black slab of Vaughan's Lincoln Continental fused with the airport tourist bus, or Catherine supine and gasping beside her upturned Mazda Miata. Even the credits have a glacial, architectural quality. The embossed chrome-effect letters mirror the deft turns of phrase that adorn the trunks of our mobile Meccas, little badges and symbols, runic inscriptions of mystical intent, decipherable only to the gnostic few who have taken time to learn this mysterious modern language.

There are two types of cinematic disaster: physical and emotional. David Lynch's *Lost Highway* is a paean to paranoia and the unwinding of the self; smalltown isolationism projected on to a city of shadows. We are unquestionably in the present, although Bill Pullman and Patricia Arquette are Modernists from another era, jarring in their (limited) interaction with the 'real' world. Their house is almost bunkerlike in its austerity; even their television is artfully propped on geometric shapes – flashes of colour in the olive-drab surroundings. Crucially, these scenes were filmed in Lynch's own home, a 1960s design by Lloyd Wright, built by his son Eric Wright during the 1980s. Lynch has spoken about his attempts to match architecture to the emotional content of his films. The sense of deconstruction is not just in the chilly interiors, but in the blasts of dislocated jazz, stroboscopically distorted, and the complex, personality-disordered plot. Buildings do not function as signifiers or location; they are fixed, frozen spaces. *Lost Highway* is Modernism's revenge – we may look sharp-edged, but those edges are razor sharp.

The lost highway of the title runs out of the city, with its random sex and violence, and into the desert. 'Rocket rocket USA, spin on down the highway', sang Suicide in 1977, neatly conflating a nation's obsession with glamour, roads and death. The journey is unceasing, the destination unknown. The *Lost Highway* motel acts as go-between for the city and its natural nemesis. This is a film of blankness and harsh shadows, red curtains, pale skin, blood-red lips and uncertain identity. Characters loom from the dark and bright light is conspicuous by its absence. Urbanism is no longer the cause of emotional trauma, it is secondary to the plot. In Lynch's world the city doesn't have to answer for society's ills; the ills adapt themselves to their surroundings.

Whether utopian or dystopian, LA is an intertextual landscape of signs that has come to represent an identifiable thread in contemporary cinema, a thread where the freeway is both god and demon, good and evil. A city simultaneously enthralled and paralysed by the car presents a bipolar portrait on screen. Disaster and architecture have colluded and collided to provide a landscape of uncertainty. We might recognise LA on the screen, but LA *noir*, the flipside of the Hollywood sign, is permanently in shadow, the rusted steel supports littered with the trash of broken lives and the legacy of self-destruction. The cinematic road, the freeway, can either take us there or far, far away.

Footnotes
1. *Los Angeles: The Architecture of Four Ecologies*, Reyner Banham, Penguin, 1990, p 35.
2. *100 Mile City*, Deyan Sudjic, p 248
3. *Los Angeles*, James Steele, Phaidon, p 11.
4. *Crash*, JG Ballard, p 49.
5. *Little Golden America: Two Famous Soviet Humorists Survey These United States*, I Ilf and E Petrov, New York, 1937, pp 76–89, quoted in *things 10*, 'Life on the Open Road: Robert Frank's *The Americans*', Summer 1999, p 32.

'America is located on a large automobile highway. When we shut our eyes and try to resurrect in memory the country, we see before us not Washington, not New York, not San Francisco, not hills, not factories, not canyons, but the crossing of two roads and a gasoline station against the background of telegraph wires and advertising billboards.' [5] △D

Cyborg Architecture

and Terry Gilliam's *Brazil*

At the start of the 21st century, with the acceleration of the dissolution between the natural body and the manufactured, whether it be technologically or genetically and medically engineered, the cyborg has become an increasingly likely and attractive proposition. Rachel Armstrong shows how, for architects, with their interest in challenging physical dimensions of existence, the fantasy of *Brazil*'s cyborg metropolis offers a startling but promising paradigm.

Above
Brazil (20th Century Fox/BFI Stills)

The term 'cyborg' broadly refers to the emerging symbiotic relationship between humans and machines and inspires a range of creative and practical disciplines that engage aesthetic, social, political and cultural investigation.

Cyborgs have become fashionable at a time when the perception of the relationship between the natural body and the 'artificial' one has been accelerated by developments in medicine and technology. New devices have woven their way into human identity so seamlessly that they are integrated into our daily functioning. In addition, the boundaries of the human body are being extruded into multiple planes.

to 'humanise' the hostile surface of the red planet. Rocks nearby the landing site of Sojourner have been nicknamed Yogi and Barnacle Bill.

The purpose of humanising the extraterrestrial environment is to extend our species' legacy. Knowing the geology of Mars, say scientists, is not only the key to understanding whether or not life exists, or has ever existed there, but also to whether this was the place where life first took hold in the solar system. According to this theory, our blue planet was 'cross-fertilised' by its red neighbour via bacteria-infested chunks of rock blasted off the surface of Mars by meteor impacts. Humans may not think of the robot as an invasion of the planet, rather that we are simply coming home.

New technologies have extended human awareness outwards into the extra-terrestrial environment. NASA has already pioneered robotic exploration techniques to expand our contact with new extraterrestrial terrains

These new projections extend both inwards into nanomolecular microcosmoses and outwards into the macrocosmos of space.

X-ray diffraction patterns and electron microscopy have magnified the interior terrains of the human body. These intimate landscapes reveal subcellular environments that are colonised by many commensals and pathogens such as bacteria and viruses. The human body can no longer be regarded as a 'pure' configuration of flesh, but is understood as a symbiotic relationship between different agencies. Where the cell itself was once regarded as the smallest unit, genetic engineering techniques have revealed that some components such as the mitochondria, the powerhouse of the cell, were once separate organisms. This subcellular 'organelle' possesses its own genetic code and has been integrated into the human membrane-bound cell structure through the process of evolution.

At the same time, new technologies have extended human awareness outwards into the extra-terrestrial environment. NASA has already pioneered robotic exploration techniques to expand our contact with new extra-terrestrial terrains. Perhaps the most endearing of these information gatherers is the Sojourner pathfinder robot, whose detailed pictures of the surface of Mars have given us the opportunity

Such 'humanisation' of alien environment and possible extra-terrestrial life forms expands the presence of humankind in the macrocosmos. By extending our ancestry into the whole history of alien life, we are claiming the entire universe as support for the evolution of Homo sapiens!

Instead of the conventional view of evolution as a consequence of Charles Darwin's 'natural selection', cyborg identities are influenced by narratives. In *The Soft Machine*, William Burroughs refers to the human body as being controlled by physical needs that can be manipulated through language. We live in an information-rich society in which we are immersed in narratives that have precipitated a visual culture where the tools for creating and communicating are predominantly visual. In the information society, the dominant language is no longer the English language but the image, and the most influential images are in the medium of film.

Film is a cybernetic structure. The celluloid strip may be considered a sort of developmental code that is read by the projector to bring to life the specific form of a moving image within a certain architecture. The cyborg architecture comes to life only when all elements are in place and the celluloid drama is enacted in front of an audience in a cinematic setting.

Even when the audience has left the auditorium, the film continues its own life. The celluloid code has been translated into the biological nervous system, becoming memories, fantasies and inspirations that will eventually influence the real world through our actions.

Cyborg bodies are influenced by their intimate inner narratives whilst remaining fully integrated with their external environments and architectures at a social and philosophical level, as well as at a physical one.

In the futuristic dystopia portrayed by Terry Gilliam's film *Brazil* (1985), the whole city, including its indigenous population, is an integrated cybernetic metropolitan system. The people sustain the informational and political systems with details of their lives that, in turn, serve to manipulate them to keep the calculated chaos of the metropolis operational. Brazil is a cannibalistic environment where human flesh and trivial data fuel the expansion of the metropolitan superorganism.

The central character, Sam Lowry, is only able to step out of the city through his vivid dreams. During the narrative, he loses his ability to distinguish between his unconcious fantasies and the metropolis, so that, effectively, he becomes a member of the audience. Once Lowry transgresses the expectations of a character in a film world, he brings the threatening world of Brazil out of the screen and into the auditorium. As he repeatedly crosses the borders between fantasy and reality, our own divisions between the film narrative and our imaginations become blurred, and the threatening consciousness of the dystopian metropolis evolves into a believable threat. Our nightmares become real.

Brazil acts through a panoramic, wholesale state-technologized surveillance system that obeys no moral code

---

Brazil is a particularly nasty entity that has a will of its own. It acts through a panoramic, wholesale state-technologised surveillance system that obeys no moral code, merely the impartial laws of 'objective' science. Every component of the cyborg metropolis that in conventional society is declared as neutral, is made active in the narrative so that computers and tape recorders, as the products of science, are an active part of the 'conspiracy'. The locus

of blame and guilt shifts cynically; the baddies are omnipresent and good guys, such as the resistance fighters who emerge from the technological guts of the metropolis, surface in the most unlikely places.

Cyborg entities are unstable due to a lack of real interconnection between the multiple systems that create them. In the hybrid structures, there are no 'natural' feedback systems that allow flesh, information and metal to mutually inform and respond to one another. The cyborg metropolis and its inhabitants are therefore always struggling with rejection of one another.

This fission is illustrated by the inhabitants' lack of concern over the perpetual terrorist blasts that beleaguer the city. They seem to expect death and rejection to be a natural part of their everyday lives, and choose to go about their daily activities as best they can whilst their cyborg city is continually being destroyed and regenerated around them.

Even the individual characters are unstable beings on the border of personal rejection or destruction. Lowry's mother employs the technologies of medicine and surgery to transgress her biological 'old age' and restore her 'original' femininity, but her body is constantly at war with the unnatural processes of 'eternal reinvention'. She suffers many surgical 'complications' and finally ends up on the floor as a gelatinous mixture of separating cyborg components. The fabric of the metropolis is also on the edge of dissolution, manifesting its systems' weaknesses through accidental detonations as deliberate acts of sabotage, as system malfunctions and information errors.

Even the outcome of the film is ambiguous: whether Lowry escapes the tyranny of Brazil's consciousness or succumbs to its systems depends on whether you are an optimist or a pessimist. The final triumph is not a cinematic one but a human one that influenced advertising and a whole generation of commercial narratives and cultural phenomena long after the film had stopped playing.

Cyborg film and architecture enjoy a unique relationship in the prevailing premillennial fear of annihilation. The shape-shifting identities that these symbiotic media convey have much to offer society. They physically and metaphorically demonstrate that it is possible to defeat obliteration, annihilation or replacement by the encroachment of the dominant patriarchal, social, technological or medical pressures on the body, and interpret them as survival techniques. They offer us a way in which to reinvent our environments and ourselves. Cyborg architects may choose film as one form of inspiration for the survival of individual creativity, and perhaps even accomplish architectural immortality by becoming part of the architecture themselves. ∆

Fantastic Spatial
Combinations in Film

The increasing capacity and widespread use of computer-generated special effects enables us to view previously unexplored combinations of space and time. Karin Damrau discusses how the architectonic potential in film to build a complex, nonlinear new reality results in such groundbreaking cinematic spectacles as the recent Smirnoff vodka advertisement, 'Smarienberg'.

Above and over page
Smarienberg
(courtesy Lowe Howard Spink).
Digital remix by Shazad Ahmed.

Film without space is inconceivable. Film stimulates us to imagine space. Even without introducing the human dimension or built structures, even when space and time are fragmented, abstracted and all scale is absent, film always articulates space. Film without a 'time-space' is also inconceivable. Space and time are always with us on those fantastic journeys in our heads that the images produce. No other form can have such a playful attitude to time and space, can compose, distort or even reinvent the interconnections between them. The question arises of how film uses this creative architectonic potential; the following are a few thoughts on the matter from my point of view as an architect.

Alongside the obvious function of architecture in film as a dramaturgic device to produce atmosphere, to intensify plot or to describe historical background, the architectonic potential of film lies in its ability to depict space and time interconnections differently from what is usual, to widen the reality we experience with its devices and to increase our sense of space. In this connection, we have to remember that it is our world-view that provides us with the basis for a new understanding of space and time and enables us to imagine space differently.

We have to accept the fact that the world we can experience with our senses is only a partial view of a multilayered reality, and that it is only with the aid of instruments that we can access a further area. It can be proved that time and space are relative and one can claim that 'space is simply a possible series of material objects and time a possible series of real events'.[1] The reality we perceive is thus only one of many possible combinations of space and time. It is this kind of realisation that forms the basis for new ideas of space.

Space need not be represented in either its logical sequence or chronologically correct order. Film devices allow us insight into new combinations of space and time, making a fantastic area of unliveable reality something we can experience. In this process, space and time are closely connected with one another; indeed, one is unthinkable without the other. Simultaneity, nonlinearity, ambiguity and complexity can be visualised through the ability of the medium to combine space and time. You can be in several places at the same time, cancel distances and visit structures that are unthinkable in the world we normally perceive.

The possibilities open to film and the methods by which it works are in themselves architectonic potential. Instead of analysing what is being represented, we should be looking more closely at film methods and techniques, as these are the board on which the game of space and time is played. The classical method of

remounting space in film is by editing the film material. As on a two-dimensional sheet of paper, new relations are established between areas of space in the collage of film material. Without having to manipulate the images themselves, spatial sequences that necessitate a new kind of orientation are possible. The viewers assemble the sequences using their imaginations, thus creating a world beyond depictable reality. In Danny Boyle's *Trainspotting* (1995), the main figure can bathe in a wonderfully clear subterranean lake by diving into the 'filthiest toilet in Scotland', and Escher's endless loops of stairs become film reality in *The Avengers* movie (Jeremiah Chechik, 1998). By using the same film sequence – the view down on to a broad staircase – several times, the film-maker can make the main actress descend the stairs without actually going down them. A labyrinth out of which there is only one way; breaking through the wall of the staircase to land urgently in everyday reality.

Until the advent of digital technologies, the possibilities open to film to form space were restricted to dealing with photographic images using analogue, collage-like, additive methods, animation techniques, varieties of exposure or even the manipulation of the film material itself.

'The camera has lost its mystifying central status as the icon of film production', as Herbert Gehr puts it.[2] He describes the deployment of the computer in film production as 'nothing more or less than the next stage in technical progress'. The computer offers the chance to generate spaces synthetically. Instead of concentrating on making the incredible credible, the computer's new potential proves to be in making the borders between photographic and synthetic space disappear. In this context, 'blurring' means softening up the actual 'interface'. The computer gently calculates a transition between two incompatible spaces; in this fashion, a hybrid of synthetic and experienced spaces is produced without a gap that has to be filled by the imagination of the viewer.

The concept of 'morphing' is relevant. Marcos Novak describes this in connection with his 'Transarchitectures' in the following fashion: 'Morphing is no longer about the mechanical juxtaposition of different objects, but rather about the alchemical admixture of different but similar fields.'[3] This means that by mixing totally new features – as far as space in film is concerned – unheard of spatial features come into being.

In a commercial for Smirnoff vodka (directed by Michel Gondry and animated by CGI specialist Pierre Buffin – who studied to be an architect) a number of these ideas were combined. A young couple are suddenly surprised by the arrival of an unpleasant

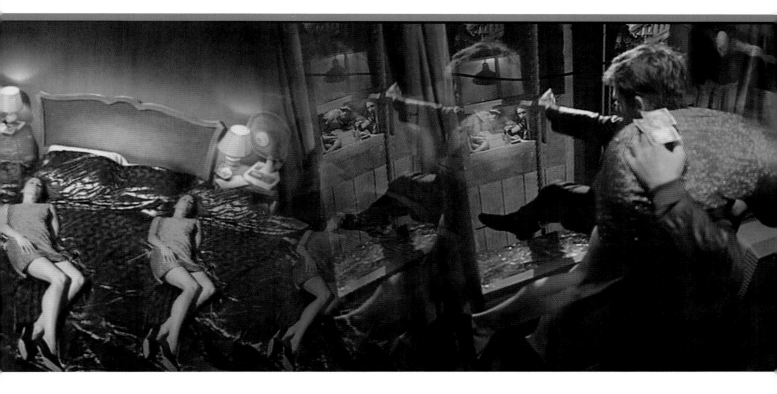

guest, and an unusual chase begins. The window through which the couple escape leads into the floor hatch of a ship; the hierarchy of top and bottom is cancelled although the couple are still subject to gravity. Floor and walls are interchangeable; it is possible to move alternately on both and their openings offer access to a known space, however impossible it is in the way it is arranged. The transition from one sequence to another is soft, spaces flow into one another and the physical laws of the single spaces overlap at the point where they join. The viewer can see how, when someone climbs through a window, the wall containing that window turns into a floor – without any kind of cut. Memories of spaces to scale, computer animation and photographic images are mixed into a hybrid, subject to its own laws and disorientating our senses, particularly when we see that the couple arrive back at their point of departure even before the chase begins.

If we think a little more about the potential of the computer, it can go far beyond generating hybrids. Spaces without scale can be created and the immaterial images need not be subject to our physical laws. What seems to be material space can flow and be in permanent movement; the relations between spaces are infinite. One might

ask whether the computer can go beyond the similarities to the reality we perceive, and generate totally new laws. Marcos Novak describes the idea of warping in this context:

> While morphing effects a fusion of pre-existing elements, warping modifies the very nature of space-time within which those elements exist... warpage...the curving of the underlying matrix itself.[4]

This allows the manipulation of the basic elements of space and hence the viewer's perception of it. If one understands film as the moving depiction of spaces, which we experience as being three-dimensional on a two-dimensional surface, whilst the images are accepted as being three-dimensional – film as an illusion of space on a plane – would it not be possible to simulate a multidimensional image on a screen? To perceive this image subject to other laws and still convey the image via a two-dimensional interface? What changed basic pattern – with its own laws and logic – would one have to feed into the computer as a starting point from which it would calculate representational models of this other world? By using all the possibilities inherent in film, and all of its technology, the medium could offer the architectonic potential to allow us to look far into the future by enabling us to immerse ourselves in previously unimaginable spaces. △○

Footnotes
1. *The Universe and Dr Einstein*, Lincoln Barnett, Mentor Books, New York, 1958, qouted in *Film as a Subversive Art*, Amos Vogel, Weidenfeld and Nicholson Ltd (London), 1974, 1997, p 14.
2. *Film & Computer*, 'Neuer Wein in alten Schläuchen?', Herbert Gehr, Deutsches Filmmuseum (Frankfurt am Main), 1998, p 17.
3. *film + arc graz 3: International Biennale*, artimage (Graz), 1997, p 74.
4. Ibid.

New Realism in Film Architecture

Fiction

The designer of a whole new generation of architectural film sets, Eric Hanson chronicles recent developments in computer-aided design in the cinema and suggests the important new role architects may take in 3-D film design. He shows examples of his work in creating large-scale digital environments for the simulation-ride film *Mars Odyssey* as well as on Luc Besson's *The Fifth Element* and Disney's new *Fantasia 2000*.

Yogi Berra once remarked, 'The future isn't what it used to be'. In the case of feature film special-effects work, this has never been so true. Film illusion techniques pioneered close to 100 years ago have remained essentially valid until just recently, when the tidal wave of digital media manipulation transformed the field. What this means for the realisation of imaginative worlds is profound, as the bar for skilful illusion has been significantly raised. New capabilities have arisen for the conveyance of rich architectural landscapes in this new and exciting period, similar to the 'golden' days of the animation explosion in the 1930s. For the cinematic-set designer or digital-effects artist, the creation of an entire world is now possible with few of the previous constraints and with more creative liaison. For the architectural designer wishing to influence the expression of architecture in film, opportunities abound, with computer-modelling techniques common to both the architecture office and film studio. This is potentially of benefit to the development of film since, with few exceptions, its rendition of the city has historically been naïve and awkward. Another realm of the architect's influence is the shaping of space within a film, a virtual but equally powerful tool to manipulate the public's perception of design.

realisation of good design. Historic films such as *Metropolis* and *Things To Come* have met this challenge, as well as more recent films such as *Blade Runner*, *Gattaca*, *The Fifth Element* and *The Phantom Menace*. An architectural sensibility can only serve to strengthen a film. Architects have long been interested in film design, but not until the digital revolution has ease of entry and the architect's potential influence in this field been so great.

The advent of CAD has provided the context for designers to work fluently in 3-D, exploring space and form freely in the infinitely malleable simulacrum of electrons. Although many were slow to adopt it initially, most firms are presently active in 3-D visualisation of design work. Whereas architects use 3-D for design exploration and purposes of client persuasion, film-effects artists utilise a similar array of digital tools to create photoreal impressions of reality. Many designers making the switch find the rules very different between the clinical perfection of pristine architectural delineation and the gritty imperfection of rendering the real world. But the techniques remain intrinsically the same, from the modelling of geometry to the detailing and painting of applied textures. Film artists generally have more time to develop their work fully compared to their architectural counterparts. Whereas the time spent detailing a building's weathered patina is crucial to the believability of a film set, for an architectural

Architects have long been interested in film design, but not until the digital revolution has ease of entry and the architect's potential influence in this field been so great.

Historically, the design of architecture in film is handled by the production designer or art director. Their primary role is to create visual form and emotional tone in the backdrop of a film. In practice though, production designers tend to be hunters and gatherers of visual material, preferring reference and assembled imagery over a methodical, iterative design process. Certainly the scope of a real-world design process would be overkill for the limited range of functions required within a film set. As a result, we are left with often banal representations of the city, with skylines almost comical in their naïveté and awkward in their massing. The production designer is as ill-equipped in these areas an architect might if called upon to frame an emotional interlude between actors. What is key, though, is the potential for film to create an uncompromised

presentation it may be frivolous, or even detrimental. Some designers entering into the film world are therefore ill-prepared for the change in emphasis in the work. Further, architects have no background in any sort of temporal media and do not have the benefit of trained cinematic pacing and cuts, so first attempts at animation tends to be painfully tedious and slow. But, the literacy of the software is often enough to enable them to gain entry to the once-cloistered profession of film-effects work. This, coupled with the fact that the field needs good designers, bodes well for those looking to make their mark in film.

Whereas CAD revolutionised the production aspect of architecture, 3-D animation has for ever altered the core of modern effects work. Rather than just supplanting existing techniques or speeding work efficiency, 3D in film has offered entirely new methods to create imagery.

Previous page
The Fifth Element (Chevannes)

Left
Mars Odyssey

The development of computer-controlled, motion-control cameras during the *Star Wars* era of the 1970s and 1980s established the present state of effects work and opened up a new vista of possibilities

Previously, environments in film were used solely to situate the action and offer establishing shots. The domination of stage shoots over location shots in the 1940s also fostered the static nature of established space, using backdrops or glass-based matte paintings to extend and fill the horizon. The development of computer-controlled, motion-control cameras during the *Star Wars* era of the 1970s and 1980s established the present state of effects work and opened up a new vista of possibilities. But, with the exception of outer space itself, this technology did little to extend descriptions of space. Matte painters still relied on glass as a substrate, with the technology opening doors only for more fluid movement of craft and objects. Motion-control did allow new manipulation of miniatures, however, and landmark films such as *Blade Runner* made good use of detailed city sets. In the late 1980s, as computer animation began to emerge from the think-tank of the original Pixar group within George Lucas' Industrial Light and Magic, certain techniques were reconsidered. Painted backdrops could now be produced with digital paint systems, offering a less toxic and more malleable format. Character work then began to be pursued, from the abstraction of the water tentacle of *The Abyss* to the fully realised dinosaurs of *Jurassic Park*. At the end of the 1990s, digital characters were omnipresent and considered

for lead roles. Whereas character work has levelled off and is now commonplace, digital sets are just beginning to reveal their potential. Films such as the *Batman* series, *Judge Dredd*, and *The Fifth Element* began to present new possibilities, but, for the sheer magnitude and ambition of its imagined worlds, the release of *The Phantom Menace* must be seen as being as pivotal for digital sets as *Jurassic Park* was for character animation.

I have had the opportunity of aiding in the development of architectural aspects in some ambitious film projects, which we will examine here. *Mars Odyssey*, a 70mm special-venue motion-based ride-film, was the first project for which a large-scale digital environment was created, with a power-of-ten flight from the bay of Tokyo to Mars and back. Working with art director Tom Valentine, I constructed an elaborate set for the earthbound segments of the film, as illustrated on page 64. A digital approach afforded the possibility of very free camera movement compared to the more rigid constraints of a motion-control/miniatures solution. One key advantage was to export the camera data out of the 3-D animation package to directly drive the hydraulics of the motion-based

seating platform. The animator could effect the sensation of motion in exact synchronicity with the visuals, and thus lessen the nausea so common in ride-film experiences. This project also encompassed a massive scale, which would have resulted in prohibitive computational demands, even with our powerful Silicon Graphics hardware. Thus, certain optimisation techniques were employed, such as painting all lighting in lieu of placing hundreds of CG light sources. Use of photographed props also helped to complete the illusion of a richly detailed industrial environment. Design references to aircraft-carrier construction were used to guide the texturing and design. Ride films, although usually trite in concept, offer rich possibilities for environmental design, as the experience is primarily concerned with moving through defined space. The current popularity of high-resolution film formats such as stereographic IMAX, coupled with the natural connection of 3-D animation software, will create novel and, hopefully, design-rich film experiences. This is an area of film history in its infancy, with landmark work waiting to be developed.

In the traditional feature-film world, digital sets offer some clear advantages over physical sets or matte paintings. In Luc Besson's *The Fifth Element*, I had the opportunity to explore some of these possibilities. Conceptually, *The Fifth Element* offered provocative

Top and middle
The Fifth Element (Chevannes)

Bottom
Fantasia 2000 (Disney)

visions of the future of Manhattan. JC Mezieres originally conceptualised a future Earth with a lowered oceanic water-table elevation, a result of exporting water to terraform distant planets. As a result, the Hudson and East rivers were run dry, establishing the island of Manhattan on a high plateau reminiscent of the Acropolis. As a corollary, real-estate development excavated down, slicing the island into vertical canyons. This changed the notion of a single street and ground plane for circulation, so hovering craft were envisioned to roam into stratified layers throughout the verticality. This alternative to the clichéd future of towering megastructures was never communicated in the script, so the rationale was quite lost on the audience. To us, at Digital Domain, however, it was a significant challenge to realise it cinematically. A solution of miniature elements and digital sets was arrived at to create the vision. A side view from Brooklyn looking across the drained East river is shown on the left. This shot is typical of the hybrid nature of effects-shot composites. Miniatures of 1960s Metabolist-inspired clusters of modular apartment units were set against a 3-D computer model of the skyline, with conventional matte painting filling in the lower reaches. The 'Thai restaurant' boat was shot as a full-size built element, its attached jet engine a 3-D computer model. The small vehicles crossing the 3-D computer model of the Brooklyn Bridge were created as 2-D painted animation and, finally, the smoke of the jet engine was rendered with a 3-D particle system. Digital animation rarely exists on its own in film; rather, most effects shots comprise the talents of many trades, all respecting the traditions of classic cinematography.

For most of the interior shots of Manhattan, miniatures were created under Mark Stetson, the visual effects supervisor on the show and original builder of the *Blade Runner* cityscape. Miniature buildings provided the clear solution for the horizontal shots looking out to the horizon. Motion-control camera rigs were used to journey through the 1:24 scale set pieces, with the camera data exported back into 3-D applications that defined the CG traffic flows. However, for a dive sequence, where the hero descends 2,000 feet down into the vertical city, we constructed a digital set to enable the length and dynamics of the move. Initial designs were nonexistent, so Ira Gilford, Tully Summers and myself looked at what might constitute the architectural nature of descending through the megalopolis. I arrived at a solution, based on the

Futurist architect Antonio Sant'Elia's sense of mass and plasticity, to anchor the lowest reaches. For the opening shot, we chose Times Square's divergent street geometry to create a more dynamic composition, shown in the smaller image on the left.

With the street layer stripped back, once-hidden infrastructures of subway shafts and city utilities are revealed, as shown on page 66. As we drop further below the daylight of street level, we begin to enter an artificially lit realm, the cacophony of Times Square, intact and independent of the time of day (shown on page 67). These backgrounds were created entirely on the computer, and offer a glimpse of what digital capabilities can provide for creating large-scale environments. In the film, the city is obscured by a maze of traffic flows, so these views depict the city more clearly. The image on pages 62/63 shows a view never seen in the film, a fanciful study image of a reflective sphere to illustrate the extreme depth of the city below. Digital sets were also used to extend partially constructed ones, a growing and economically advantageous use of the technology.

Another notion is the merging of a live-action set with partial digital elements. In *Fantasia 2000*, Disney's follow-up to the celebrated original of the 1940s, I·had the opportunity to help design the backdrop for the Interstitial segments – the introductions to each piece of animation. Intending to maintain the spirit of abstraction of the original *chiaroscuro* of orchestra members silhouetted against coloured backdrops, we chose to create a modern scrim of curvilinear forms to deflect and modulate the projected shadows, as seen oppposite. With the addition of motion, colour, and transparency, the sails represent a vestige of the original, but carry a contemporary design influence. For the final production, an orchestra was filmed on a built physical stage floor, with the background sails produced digitally in a seamless union of the two. This fulfilled the notion of an abstract, timeless realm in which the performance takes place. The project suggests the potential of computer graphics to create abstract and surreal environments, the realisation of which would be limited by physical techniques.

New digital techniques have altered our media for ever, and offer rich possibilities for the new breed of digitally literate designers to explore exciting new realms of expression and realism. Just as the real effect and ramifications of new technologies could never be predicted during the 20th century, it is interesting to speculate on where this new Prospero-like power of imagination might lead. If Hollywood's abysmal reliance on spectacle over content diminishes and does not circumvent the real potential of digital imagery, we are in for interesting film experiences as we enter the new millennium. Skilled architectural designers would do well to help lead this exploration. △

The Development of the Modernist Cinema

Sideshow to Art House

Edwin Heathcote investigates the history of
the cinema building, from fairground booth
to the avant-garde. In discussing Coop
Himmelb[l]au's ufa Palast in Dresden, Avery
Associates' imax at Waterloo, London and
Saucier + Perotte's Cinemathèque Québecoise
in Montreal, he argues for the crossing over
of filmic space and space for film, where
cinema design should reflect the diverse visual
wealth contained within the most imaginative
architecture for film and the true colour
and vulgarity of its own populist roots

Cinema is often seen as the only truly 20th-century art form. Fine art in galleries, despite attracting audiences greater than those for football matches, remains a middle-class pursuit. Modern classical music and jazz have lost their appeal to all but die-hard enthusiasts. Poetry is little read, literature a little more so. Architecture has split into camps but its avant-garde remains resolutely bent over double, gazing long and hard into its own navel, even though it seems to be slowly returning from the exile imposed in the wake of the failure of tower blocks and flat roofs. It is certainly the most popular and is one of the few artistic media that manages to transcend class, education and cultures. Cinema, like jazz, architecture and art has its fringes and its avant-garde, and intellectuals invest it with complex meanings, yet it has not lost its popular edge. In this, it has remained true to its original role as a pure source of entertainment and wonder.

The roots of the moving picture lie not in the 20th century but in the 19th-century fairground. The early cinemas were coarse booths, which were assembled and disassembled in

potential of film but few looked to the cinema building itself. This unwillingness to accept the architecture of the cinema as a serious genre remains prevalent; film is still seen as diversionary entertainment for the masses and, while theatres are given grants and huge public subsidies, cinemas are, on the whole, left to fend for themselves. They are thought to be commercially viable and not in need of the same kind of assistance. The result has been the destruction of a huge number of buildings from the 1930s and the construction of enormous complexes of industrial sheds housing gargantuan multiplexes showing only a few Hollywood blockbusters on all their many screens. Only recently has a younger generation of architects, who grew up submersed in popular culture and the images of the screen, begun to regard the cinema as a serious and indispensable contribution to the urban fabric.

One of the persistent problems facing cinema architects is that of expression. What is to be expressed? The cinema is one of the most inward-looking of buildings, which focuses on a screen that remains unseen from the outside. Apart from the auditorium, there is the lobby to think of, and this may or may not interact with its urban context. In the 1930s, the cinema interior was seen as a place of escape,

There is none of the nobility or the grandiose permanence of the Ancient Greek theatre in the cinema as a building type

fairgrounds. There is none of the nobility or the grandiose permanence of, say, the ancient Greek theatre in the genesis of the cinema as a building type. The first to see the potential of film were entrepreneurs who set up these booths or converted existing theatres or church halls to show short films designed to thrill, shock and titillate. Neither the films nor the wonderfully tacky buildings set up to display them were considered art. This was cheesy fairground nonsense, not to be taken seriously. Pioneer directors, however, quickly began to see the possibilities of the moving picture and narrative, plot, jumps in time and other devices employed to create a new artistic world. But the architecture of the cinema continued to be viewed as disposable and ephemeral; not worthy of great attention. Until the 1930s, when some wonderful cinemas were built, only the Russian Constructivists, with their love of agitprop and the dismountable architecture of permanent revolution, saw the possibilities of cinema architecture as a means to reach the masses. Most 20th century artistic movements, from the Surrealists to the Pop artists, saw the

a fantasy world within which the worker could feel part of the Hollywood visions of Busby Berkeley or the sumptuous Art Deco settings of a Fred Astaire picture. The architecture provided a fantasy a world apart from the unemployment and slums without. Art Deco began as a rich French decadent style and spread to become a language of escapism, the architecture of bars, hotels and cinemas. Just as the Gothic cathedral was seen as a kind of foretaste of heaven for the illiterate masses of medieval Europe, a trailer for the forthcoming attraction, so the cinema provided a glimpse into another world, a world of beauty, dancing, music and escape.

War, the Holocaust and the Cold War stripped away some of these cinematic illusions; Neo-Realism emerged from Italy and bleak kitchen-sink dramas came out of England; cinema as escapism was on the retreat, now the reserve of Hollywood musicals. This fundamental change spread through to cinema architecture, and the postwar years in which Modernism truly took hold of the architectural establishment saw little action in the building of new cinemas. In fact, the most significant cinematic building-type to emerge during the Cold War years was the antibuilding of the drive-in, a glorified car park or lovers' lane.

Opposite and above
Coop Himmelb(l)au's
UFA Palast, Dresden

71

The emergence of Postmodernism in the 1970s and 1980s saw an increasing recognition of the forms and archetypes of popular culture and an acknowledgment of the importance of the visual, while cinema entered the realms of philosophy as a subject for serious consideration, particularly in France where the intellectual standing of film has remained consistently high. After the puritanism of Modernism, it was as if Rococo had broken out again, and cinemas, along with multimedia and cultural centres, re-emerged to take their place at the heart of the community where the theatre or the church may once have stood. The fragmentation and deconstruction that has emerged as the dominant avant-garde of recent years is closely related to the staggered, illusory nature of filmic time and space, which has led to a change in the perception of the cinema as an experimental building-type. Certainly, the most graphic recent representation of this crossing over of filmic space and space for film is Coop Himmelb(l)au's UFA Palast in Dresden.

Its architects see the cinema not so much as a building but a container of public space. Its crystalline form, which echoes the works of the Czech Cubists and the German Expressionists of the interwar period, allows a series of views and visible routes through the building from the public realm, but at the same time, it fragments and distorts those routes and views, as does a camera. This fragmented use of space coincides with Coop Himmelb(l)au's approach to the urban fabric, which is based around the notion that the solid and void, gridlike nature of cities is defunct, and that the future will see buildings being used as permeable, multifunctional interventions on a site, containing both internal and public circulation routes. In some ways, this use of space will see the return of the cinema lobby as a social space at the centre of urban activity. With eight screens, this building should be classified as a multiplex, a cinema-type typified by an anti-urban, anti-architecture. However, it

is located near the centre of Dresden, a city that was flattened by Allied bombing and rebuilt in a manner lacking in the traditional density of European city centres. This fragmentation and lack of spatial and architectural cohesion makes it the ideal venue for the practice's experiments with new types of urban space. There is also a kind of operatic bravado attached to the scheme – an attention-seeking aesthetic that is entirely appropriate to the entertainment values of the movies. This theatricality is enhanced at night when the building becomes a glowing crystal, its circulation guts exposed to the city.

The stage-set qualities continue within the glass shell as a series of highly Mannerist architectural gestures that clarify the unreality of the filmic medium: stairs that end suddenly, going nowhere, a twisted tower containing a lift (which has to have a straight trajectory) and suspended sculptural forms. All of these enhance the three dimensionality of the space, contrasting with the two dimensions of the film clips that are projected throughout the public areas of the building as well as on the screens themselves. It has by no means been a universally popular building. Sharp corners and plunging planes have caused safety concerns and some are now covered in high-visibility plastic sheeting, while the standard of construction and finishing has brought criticism. These problems, however, do not conspire to mute the effect of this dramatic building, which will inevitably exert a powerful influence on the (rather limited) realm of avant-garde cinema architecture.

Coop Himmelb(l)au's cinema reveals a chaotically collapsing space; the crumpled and sometimes awkward interior is slightly (and deliberately) oppressive. Koen van Velsen's new cinema in Rotterdam is a purer variation on a similar theme of cinema as light-box illuminating an incoherent public realm, but this is a pre-crumpling building; a vision of modern purity before it has been put through the de-con crusher. The translucent shell of van Velsen's cinema is more apparent at night, when it glows from within, the auditoria appearing as solid masses in a diaphanous wrapping. Simple, light and elegant it maintains a hierarchical urban relationship, similar to that of a freestanding theatre, with the large plaza in front; a dramatic building at the centre of an entertainment district. In this way, both the cinema and the area outside become theatrical spaces and, in contrast to the Coop Himmelb(l)au scheme, public and semi-public spaces are clearly delineated. The plaza is 24-hour, the circulation is partly restricted access and the two work together without any pretence of abandoning traditional spatial distinction.

Avery Associates' new IMAX cinema in London's Waterloo is a simple carousel. It could be snidely argued that its circus form reflects the fairground nature of the IMAX format, which, although undoubtedly impressive, is having trouble being accepted into the wider world of film. The site for the IMAX, a grim hole at the centre of a roundabout that was formerly the hub of London's homeless community, is unpromising. It is hard, in fact, to see what else the architect could have done. With the nearby arts ghetto of London's South Bank Centre dominated by rainstained and largely unpopular concrete blocks, the bright splash of colour of Patrick Hodgkinson's abstract decoration, which adorns the drum, acts as a welcome diversion. Brian Avery adopts the same transparency and lightness within a firmly High-Tech architectural language that he used for his inventive and low-budget Museum of the Moving Image, a short walk away. The IMAX undoubtedly acts as a successful hub and a visual marker in a desolate concrete subtopia, but it is a simplistic response. The platonic cylinder suggests an interior of Colosseum-like proportions or perhaps a surround screen.

The IMAX adopts a tight transparency and lightness within a firmly high-tech architectural language

In fact the auditorium is disappointingly traditional and, although impressively large, lacks the Roman grandeur implied by its shell. On the other hand, the High-Tech lightness of the glazed drum, the lurid colours of the (changeable) painting and the transparency and suggestion of building itself as screen begin to work as a formula for an expressive architecture of the cinema, building on the medium's side-show roots. It echoes

the precursors of the cinemas: the panoramas, dioramas and globes of the 19th century, utterly appropriate to the IMAX format, which aims to instill awe and to overwhelm with scale and depth.

The Cinemathèque Québecoise in Montreal by Saucier+Perrotte, like Avery's IMAX cinema is placed in a tight and constrictive context, but in a more urban situation. It embraces a diverse combination of functions, including two cinemas, an archive, a film school, the omnipresent café and a series of public galleries, encompassing an existing school building at its centre. The architects have squeezed the elements of a complex brief onto the site and the result is architecturally exciting. There is a definite sense of the filmic in the fragmentary nature of the glimpsed spaces, a kind of sharp editing that constantly leads the eye into the next scene. Like the Coop Himmelb(l)au cinema, the cinemathéque invites and leads the public through a series of involving spaces including an elegant courtyard, and the building's partial transparency proves tantalising. A screen on its front is used to project images into the public realm of the street, while behind the screen a long band of glazing exposes the activity within. The centre is very much about projecting to the city as well as to the internal screens.

Of these buildings, it is undoubtedly the Dresden cinema that is the most striking and powerful as an image. The others featured here are certainly sophisticated, but there is something brash and attention-seeking in Coop Himmelb(l)au's cinema, which is perhaps the truest to the fairground origins of the cinema booth – it represents a kind of helter-skelter ride comparable to the capability of film to play with the viewer's position in time, space and emotion. Yet it strikes me that all these buildings occupy a position in the city similar to that of the theatre or the arts centre, and that the notion of a distinct cinema architecture is still in genesis. Bearing in mind the popularity and near universality of cinema-going, this seems curious. There seems to be inspiration in the vulgarity, the impermanence of the early cinemas as transient structures, which has not yet been fully tapped. Perhaps the most successful and memorable use of architecture in film is the Expressionistic sets for *The Cabinet of Dr Caligari* (1919), in which the action is based around a fairground booth, or cabinet, and the murderous potential of its somnambulist inhabitant. It seems to me that the further development of cinema architecture needs to draw on the most imaginative architecture for film and on its own populist, background. Something of the absurd, lunatic, Expressionistic thrill needs to be retained in the architecture of the cinema if it is to express the scope, range and power of what can be seen within. Δ

Opposite
Saucier + Perrotte Architects'
Cinematheque Quebecoise

Above
Avery Associates' IMAX Cinema

Cinematic Scarpa

Film director Murray Grigor, who has previously made documentaries on Charles Rennie Mackintosh and Frank Lloyd Wright, writes of his pursuit to 'find the cinematic means to reveal something of the rich sensory experience that visitors feel as they journey through a building by Carlo Scarpa'. Grigor's clarity of purpose meant that the project almost failed to find funding as he eschewed the usual documentary film conventions such as the journalistic voice-over.

'The trouble with you English is that you see with your ears', the great Neo-Classicist sculptor Antonio Canova told the delegation of *Inglese* who had travelled to Italy to commission a sculpture from him. 'You are only capable of seeing what you're told to see. Your own Flaxman is the first sculptor in Europe and you don't know it. Give him your commission.'

Those words had a particular resonance on the day we laid out our tracks to film the plaster casts of Canova's sculptures in the incomparable space that the architect Carlo Scarpa had created for them in the late 1950s, next to the the sculptor's studio in Possagno. For those who believe that being told what to see is quite a different experience from seeing what is shown, the idea of a 'show' rather than 'tell' film on Scarpa's architecture had been a formidably difficult project to finance.

Working around the usual funding agencies, we had come near to an advance from *Arte la Sept* in Paris, whose imaginative commissioning editor Thierry Garrel not only knew our subject well but also had his own idea of commissioning a film without words on Scarpa's most enigmatic work, the Brion tomb on the Veneto. But that fell through because Thierry was refused essential co-production money from one of Britain's best-known commissioning editors of art documentaries. 'How can viewers comprehend what you're showing them without a journalist on screen explaining what they're seeing?' 'In France', Thierry replied with a wry smile, 'we would call that radio'.

Nonetheless, we held to the notion that if we could find the cinematic means to reveal something of the rich sensory experience that visitors feel as they journey through a building by Carlo Scarpa, such a film could be a revelation to a wide television audience. Although Scarpa's work was never in the mainstream of contemporary architecture and his craft-based detailing was considered an anachronistic irrelevance in machine-led Modernism, books were now stacking up on his work. By the beginning of the 1990s, Scarpa was rediscovered as an architect's architect, especially for his work in museum restoration in heritage-obsessed Britain.

If our film could not only give flight to Scarpa's mastery of space and light but also reveal how he invested the historical objects in his spaces with meaning, we might even influence the way in which important redundant buildings are restored in the future.

Unlike most recently adapted historical buildings, where much that has been added is often conjectural and sometimes clearly bogus, Scarpa left no confusion between what is old and new. He created a tension between the surviving fabric and his newly devised parts. The idea of 'fitting in' for Scarpa was a falsification of history. In his restorations, you are never confused as to where you are in history. The past is always distinct from the present. In essence, Scarpa was beyond fashion. Would it be possible to make a film that itself was out of fashion? Could such a film articulate Scarpa's notion of a design journey? If we could add to this something of the enthusiasm and recollections that so many of Scarpa's craftworkers and assistants still held for their beloved maestro, we might even be able to make something truly memorable.

After five years of plugging away, it would be the now disbanded but then culturally proactive film department of the Arts Council of England, along with Channel 4 that would make our film possible, topped up by the generosity of the Dunard Fund through the Canadian Centre for Architecture. With the architect and Scarpa scholar Richard Murphy as my guide, we set out for Venice to select what to film and to meet as many of the late maestro's collaborators as possible.

'Why do you want to make a film on this most Venetian of Italian architects?' asked the architect Luciano Gemin, one of his last assistants. We were in Scarpa's favourite restaurant, just off a canal near the palace of the Fondazione Querini Stampalia, which he had so creatively remodelled in the early 1960s. I explained that my first film had been on Charles Rennie Mackintosh and that I had since made one on Frank Lloyd Wright; two of Scarpa's greatest mentors. The foundation's director, Giorgio Busetti, peered back at me across the table, cradling a tiny dog with darting inquisitive eyes. 'For me, this film on Carlo Scarpa', I tentatively suggested, 'would complete the trinity'. 'Bellissimo', exclaimed Gemin, throwing his arms in the air. Our project was off to a flying start.

Emerging from under the waters of the lagoon, our film would open in Venice, the floating city, for here was the wellspring of Scarpa's imagination. Everything he designed seemed to flow back in its inspiration to the Venice where he grew up. 'I am a man of Byzantium', he once offered as his epitaph, 'who came to Venice by way of Greece'. Venice seemed to inform his architecture at every turn. We aimed to show how the transparency and mobility of water inspired his designs. We would refract his architecture through the Venice of his memories: the bright unexpected colours glimpsed out of darkness; the sudden glint of gold in the shadows; the intricacy of

ornament and inlay work; the switches in scale of views; the contraction and expansion of spaces. So many of these visual experiences are evoked in his masterful remodelling of the Querini Stampalia. Here, we would show how Scarpa carved out a whole gallery space and lined it with slabs of travertine like the exterior-clad walls of a Venetian *palazzo*. An extra-large notched slab moved under Richard's hand to become a door, inspired by the stone shutters Scarpa had always admired on the ancient church on the Venetian island of Torcello.

In the derelict, unloved backyard, Scarpa created a garden, where a series of water channels and architectural details crisscross a lawn. The skies opened on the day we chose to film it. Great sheets of rain plummeted down, creating overlapping rings in the pools and causing the stalks of bamboos to bend in waving patterns like a Japanese woodcut. Now we had a sequence that was the perfect expression of Scarpa's love of the Orient, conveyed without words. Ripples turned through right angles and rushed down the concrete conduits, as a geometric microcosm of Venice's meandering canals. The poured concrete retaining walls, laid in graded layers like fossil sediments of time, held a narrow band of brightly coloured tiles, which glistened as we filmed them in the rainy half-light. They seemed to sing of the forces of past and present, of erosion and new construction; an almost infinite interplay of Venetian themes ebbing around water.

'Thinking of water flowing around the walls', said Scarpa when he came to remodel the Castelvecchio museum in Verona, 'gave me the idea of edging the floors in a different material'. From a low angle, we showed how channels of local prun stone now run around rafts of polished concrete, which appear to float from gallery to gallery, unifying the ground floor back to a gridded gate in the far distance. Scarpa was anxious to reveal the complex history of this ancient building. In the Napoleonic period, a barrack block had been erected next to the medieval fortress. A hundred years later, it had been decked out as a fictional palace, complete with false beams and elaborate decoration as a rather confusing background for the genuine art on display. It was all too much like the remodelling of Windsor Castle. Stripping out the dummy beams, Scarpa saw that they served a function in connecting the galleries visually and this inspired one of his most heroic solutions. Our

camera craned up to reveal what Scarpa had devised – a massive, centrally positioned, riveted steel girder running from one gallery to the next. Instead of pastiche, Scarpa brought his own 20th-century vocabulary of forms to complement what had survived from the past. His primary aim was to allow art and architecture to play off one against the other – creating a meaningful journey through the complex history of the castle.

Scarpa took infinite care in positioning the sculptures in these galleries. He wanted the viewer and object to meet on a one-to-one basis. This was a radical, democratic concept at a time, following Mussolini's vision of museums, when the people were invited to stand in awe of the treasure hoards of the state. Scarpa instead lures you to look in a series of directed gazes; invites you to take a predetermined journey and nudges you into making meaningful connections from one object to another. In setting up a tracking shot, we had the chance of slowing down this act of looking; of directing gazes; of dwelling on incidents to stress those connections. We fixed on a small Madonna held out on an iron armature in one room and then slowly revealed the anguished Christ that Scarpa positioned so movingly under a shaft of sunlight in the gallery beyond. In film-making, time can be collapsed. We are free to select from a day the most telling light.

Scarpa encourages viewers to move around the exhibits. We included an excerpt from a RAI film of the 1960s in which Scarpa swivels us back on our heels to view a sculpture from behind. And then we matched his point of view in the gallery to reveal the same impeccably arranged group of sculptures under a different light. In Scarpa's design, works of smaller scale were also given their special place. Small sculptures were set against screens and clasped in steel armatures fabricated in the Zanon workshop. There was that Madonna again, now revealed against a wide screen of shimmering red stucco *lucido*, a marble-like plaster made by a process that was rediscovered under Scarpa's eye by the Venetian plasterer Eugenio de Luigi.

As an assistant slapped the mixture of coloured plaster and marble dust up and down with a broad spatula, there was Eugenio flicking through a book on Rothko's paintings. Where else in the world would a plasterer refer to Abstract Expressionist art to check the intensity of his colours? But then, this was Venice and Eugenio had seen a Rothko exhibition at the Biennale. Nearby, in the Zanon Brothers' metal workshops, Francesco drilled into a steel plate and then slipped in a little collar of brass; a contrast of bright yellow against the black metal, called for by Scarpa to celebrate the process of making the joint. Francesco, in his rapid-fire speech revealed how Scarpa could not only draw with both hands, but

could also create two quite separate designs.

Of all Scarpa's creative interventions at the Castlevecchio it would be his imaginative solution to the siting of Verona's greatest equestrian sculpture that would be his most astonishing design feat. All the histories of the castle coincide at the pivotal point where Scarpa chose to place the *Cangrande della Scala*, or the 'Great Dog of the Stair', as the Renaissance prince Scaligeri was nicknamed. Here, Scarpa severed the Napoleonic roof from the medieval fortress wall, exposing the sky in right-angled sections. Underneath, he created a great concrete plinth and a variety of viewing levels to display the triumphant *Cangrande*. The architect, Arrigo Rudi, was choked with emotion as he rhapsodised about how his master Scarpa had created this great rotational space. 'I believe', Rudi said, 'when you cross this part of the museum, you can feel in a very emotional way all the history of the town. The presence of the master – the *Cangrande*.' As Rudi explained how elements from all periods of the castle's history had been triumphantly exposed here by Scarpa, our shots cut from above to below to the sides and then rose to a climax of Jonathan Dove's music towards the great *Cangrande* as he flared out from the sun, revealing in close-up his famous, enigmatic smile.

The same plummeting rains that had drenched with meaning our filming in the garden of the Querini Stampalia had covered a field outside the little village of San Vito d'Altivole with a huge pond of water. The low walls and cypresses of the Brion tomb now loomed across a reach of water in the early morning light, like a vision from Bocklin's *Island of the Dead*. Guiseppe Brion was the founder of the innovative electronics giant Brion Vega. Could he ever have imagined that his posthumous fame would now rest on this extraordinary memorial to him in the little village cemetery where he was born? What Scarpa built here remains one of the great enigmas of contemporary architecture. Is it his answer to that age-old question: can architecture be poetry? 'I wanted to create,' Scarpa said, 'a garden of meditation, peaceful, pagan, a place to visit the dead without the shoeboxes of a village cemetery'.

For Scarpa time was never money. Beginning in 1969, he spent almost ten years on the construction of the Brion tomb. It is now a place of pilgrimage for architects from all over the world, especially from Japan. Sadly, there must have been grave robbers among them for many

of Scarpa's exquisite details in complex combinations of wood and metal have been stolen over the years. For our film, the brothers Anfodillo and Zanon remade certain elements for the chapel, including the long pendant candelabrum.

Stefano Biscaro and Dario Guardi, our resourceful grip and gaffer, took up the challenge to put the clogged-up water conduits and broken pulleys back to work. Suddenly, there was the sound of bubbling water. Once again, there was that narrow stream of water flowing down towards Scarpa's broad lake of meditation as a river of life. With much perseverance, the complex door-lifting mechanism of bobbins and pendulum weights, which Scarpa had devised against the shuttered concrete wall on the outside, was set to work again. '*Viva Italia!*' shouted Stefano from above. Now the pulleys whirled when Brion's son Ennio pressed down the internal glass gate, allowing him to make his pilgrimage on to the lake of meditation. Ennio's eyes were caught for a moment, clasped in the twin cusps of a vignette, directing his gaze back to the arches over his parents' tomb and the little village beyond Scarpa's sloping buttressed walls. Ennio sat down and pondered. What words were necessary now? All we heard were the sounds of lapping water, buzzing insects, the cry of a crow and the distant toll of the village church. In the end, Scarpa leaves visitors to bring their own meanings to his multiple forms, which pivot on the cycle of life and death in this sacred grove.

'When would the work be finished?' the villagers asked. 'When it's finished it will be dead', Scarpa replied. It never was completed. Plans for further work like a boat to sail the lake of meditation would never be realised. For while visiting his beloved Japan in 1978, Scarpa fell down a flight of steps and died. He had chosen for himself a place between the Brion tomb and the little square plots of the village cemetery. His grave is in the corner, where once the dead flowers were thrown. 'I shall rest here in no-man's-land', he said, 'in the municipal copse'. This seemed the place to end our film, before dissolving back into the water and revealing once again the bustle of life on a canal in Venice.

The Architecture of Carlo Scarpa, directed by myself with photography by Terry Hopkins and music by Jonathan Dove, went on to open the Festival of Films on Art in Montreal and was a key part of the Scarpa exhibition, *Intervening with History*, which ran until the end of October 1999 at the enterprising Canadian Center for Architecture in the same city. Although the Scarpa film was produced in 1996, it is already something of a historical document. The great Venetian cabinetmaking firm of the Anfodillo Brothers has since closed its doors on the Canareggio. ∆

All images
16 mm offcuts from
*The Architecture
of Carlo Scarpa*

Building Films

The director Karl Sabbagh makes documentaries about architecture. His work often features more construction workers than architects, concerned with the entire process of producing a building rather than just its design. Currently, he is working on a five and a half year project covering the story of Herzog and de Meuron's Tate Gallery at Bankside.

The most interesting thing to me about architecture is not the drawings themselves but how they are transformed – often radically – as they are turned into buildings. That's why the films I make are often about architecture only 10 per cent of the time and about all sorts of other interesting things to do with buildings for the other 90 per cent.

I have often thought that the job of a team making a building is similar to a television production team, and as the producer/director I play a similar role to the architect. So I know very well the dilemmas and disappointments as crisp, elegant plans turn into a disappointing mishmash. We both make things that are judged from the outside. Few people know about the bones beneath the skin – of buildings as well as television programmes – and yet those are just as important.

In architecture, as in film production, some of what happens, and some of what makes a work memorable, surprising or distinctive, is down to seizing opportunities that present themselves as a result of random occurrences. And in both cases, technology plays a part – in architecture, the malleability of steel, the friability of clay, the expansion of glass; in film, the reaction of emulsion to light, of iron particles to magnetism, the ability of a video camera to keep recording for 40 minutes without interruption, compared with a film camera, which can only hold 10 minutes of film.

Architects occasionally appear in my films, but so do demolition experts, project managers, mechanical engineers, tenants, developers, lift engineers, metallurgists and anyone else whose job or situation might bring them into contact with a building. I think, however, that the films I make may tell people more about architecture and architects than many films that begin and end with the job of the architect. Often, in fact, they begin and end with just one part of the job of an architect: the conception of the exterior envelope of a building.

Over the years, I have developed a working method that has revealed much to the television audience – and even to people in the business – about how buildings are made. It is based on a surprisingly freewheeling approach to the topic, and the belief that you can arrive at the truth about your subject by a whole variety of different routes, many of which are equally valid. Be flexible, undogmatic and opportunistic and you may get much nearer to the truth of an unfolding series of events than if you study

the subject hard beforehand, come to a conclusion and then make a film that fits that conclusion.

In 1994, the Tate Gallery in London announced a competition to find an architect to design a new space, using the existing fabric and site of the disused Bankside power station. The commissioning editor of arts programmes for Channel 4 asked my company to make a documentary series that would follow the process from the competition to the opening of the new gallery in the year 2000. We made one programme, which went out in November 1996, as an introduction to the project, and are now filming for about a day a month to gather material that will enable us to tell the story of the project. My approach to those filming days gives some insight into how my programmes evolve.

If a filming day supplies only what I imagined it would and no more, I will be disappointed. I make a point of trying to avoid pre-planning sequences, preferring to film whatever happens on the day I have chosen. I may have been told that a particular event will take place on the day, and then discover when I arrive that it happened yesterday, or will happen tomorrow. But, almost as often, I find things that I hadn't expected and that may be equally interesting.

Diary of a filming day: Eight o'clock on an autumn morning in London. We are outside Bankside power station. There's me, a cameraman Colin Rogal, a sound recordist Andy Cottom, an assistant Phil Penfold, and my PA Gillian Faulkner. We are there to capture architecture in the raw.

The task I set myself on filming day is often a simple one: to record what happens. The choices I make are more to do with when to film than what. Many documentary-makers work to a script. The task I set myself – capturing what happens – is both easier and more difficult than this. It is easier because I have little or no control over what goes on in front of the camera and therefore my opportunities for intervention as a director are limited. I take a chance that on the day I choose to film there will be a series of events – some that would take place anyway, such as site activity, meetings, ceremonies and so on and some prearranged by me, such as interviews with specific people or filming from a vantage point where access has to be organised beforehand. The most interesting footage from a specifically televisual point of view comes out of the events that would happen anyway. With the help of a miniaturised microphone that can be clipped to a participant, someone who is going about his everyday work can be followed at a distance by the camera, while his conversations are relayed by radio on to the tape. This sort of filming usually produces footage that allows me to tell a tiny part of the story in great detail.

In the Tate Bankside project, significant events were

taking place every day in Basel, on Millbank, in Camden Town, in Bankside itself, as well as in the heads of the main participants, who could be in any of these places or on a plane to Los Angeles. So my films, like all documentaries, are con tricks. They try to convey the impression that I have been everywhere and made a careful selection of the most important events, whereas in fact I have been to 1 per cent of the places and use those occasions to tell the story. The omission of events that I don't cover will – I hope – never be noticed, since the audience don't know what they're missing.

This is a lesson I have learnt the hard way, and it may have relevance for architecture as well. People spend time and emotional effort defending the retention of elements whose absence no one will notice if they are not in the final product. I have spent many hours in cutting rooms and edit suites consoling – or browbeating – neophyte producers who have grown attached to sequences that have to be dropped to get the programme down to length. In the end, there is only one question to ask: in order to keep this sequence in the programme will a better sequence have to go? (Better in a whole variety of senses to do with the structure of the programme, the storytelling, the pace and texture and so on.) If the answer is 'yes' then the sequence goes out. Now clearly, the situation is slightly different in a building. But there are constraints that are analogous to the duration of a programme – cost, height, safety – where choices have to be made to leave things out that the architect would really like to have included. Provided what's left in is good enough, nobody misses what isn't there.

The film will show how the combination of technology, planning and chance combine to provide the ingredients for a documentary about architecture

A visit to the construction management offices coincides with a visit by a small group from the Tate team, including Peter Wilson, the Tate's Director of Buildings and Services, a key figure in the design process. I notice some large grilles leaning against a filing cabinet. At previous meetings and during interviews with team members, I've heard a certain amount of discussion about the design of the floor grilles and I decide to talk to Wilson about the current situation.

However well budgeted a series is, one is unlikely to be able to afford to film on more than a fraction of the days during which the key events happen and in more than a fraction of the important locations. But you can give an impression of omniscience and of having been in all the important places at the right times by selecting a single aspect of the story and following it in some detail. You choose one component of a building, for example, and follow it from drawing board to opening day. If you've made the right choice of component the story will illustrate much wider issues to do with the building as a whole – the way decisions are made, the constraints of budget and schedule, the behaviour of materials in different conditions, conflicts between engineering and architecture, running costs of the finished building, maintenance issues and so on.

This was in my mind when I decided on impulse to talk to Wilson about the grilles. There had already been an interesting issue early on in the design process about which type of heating and ventilation system to use.

I asked Peter Wilson if he had time for an interview. Although he was about to have a meeting, he agreed to stand by the grilles and answer a few questions. Wilson: 'It's all to do with having decided to use displacement air conditioning, which has to be delivered through the floor. And in order to convince ourselves and our curatorial colleagues that there was a design strategy that would make the grilles less obtrusive, we hit upon this notion that they've got to be heavy and substantial. The whole inspiration for this kind of pattern of grilles comes from the kind of cast radiator grilles that we have at (the Tate Gallery at) Millbank, which, in spite of the fact that they're obtrusive because they're in the centre of rooms, are not obtrusive as objects in their own right, and tend to disappear, and so that's where we started from. And in this case "unobtrusive" always means consistent, it never means invisible, because even minimalist architects produce things that are quite visible.'

Impromptu interviews like this one are often livelier and more interesting than the set-piece interview carried out in someone's office. Somehow, standing in your overcoat in the middle of an office with other people going about their work, phones ringing and general office noise in the background leads to something more like a conversation than an interview.

The impression of informality is reinforced by shooting with a hand-held camera perched on the shoulder of the cameraman, rather than the more formal camera on a tripod. In this case, the approach was very rewarding since it led to a succinct disquisition on the recent thinking of the team about much broader issues of style for the whole building, as well as illuminating the big picture through the small details of decision-making about the grilles.

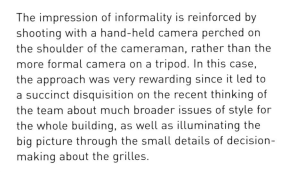

During the morning, while filming on the roof, I had noticed a deafening rumble every few minutes as workmen with wheelbarrows carried the rubble they had created and tipped it down a chute to the floor of the power station 200 feet below. I made a mental note to shoot the other end of the sequence later that day, and in the afternoon, we assembled on the floor to film the long segmented chute as it snaked around under the force of the tumbling blocks and dust before depositing them on a growing pile on the floor. As load after load came down the chute we filmed it in all shot sizes and angles: a wide shot; a pan down the tube as the rubble dropped; a midshot of the end of the chute as the rubble came through; a tight shot of the end of the tube; and a shot of the pile of rubble as another load was added to it.

In all, we probably had ten different angles, of which we might use two or three in the final programme. Or none. It is always possible that, in spite of its value as a sequence in which actual movement occurs – something quite rare in programmes on architecture – it will never appear in the final programme.

This is a tiny example of something that happens all the time, on a much bigger scale. By definition, if you film 250 hours or so of material for a four-hour series, 98 per cent or so is never used. But it is impossible to identify the 2 per cent that is best for the programme until you have all the material in front of you and until you know the programme you want to make, which is based on how the story turns out.

In the late afternoon we returned to the exterior of the building to shoot a particular type of shot of which I am fond. I call it a 'registered mix' and it's often useful in architecture sequences when you want to show the progress that has been made in some comparatively slow process construction or demolition, usually. In this case, we had filmed the ground-level buildings that were due to be demolished on a shoot the previous month and had a wide shot of the predemolition scene. Now, with half the buildings gone, I wanted another shot that was filmed from exactly the same spot with exactly the same lens, angle and framing.

I planned to take another identical shot on the next shoot, after the buildings had disappeared entirely. In the editing, I could dissolve slowly between these three shots and create the effect of the outbuildings dissolving, emphasising how the architects' vision of a clean envelope was being achieved.

It was now about 6.00 pm. We had been working for a fairly normal ten hours or so, and had shot three 40-minute cassettes worth of material, quite a low amount for me, mainly because we had only one interview – the short chat with Peter Wilson – and no meetings. Excluding any producer/director costs or office overheads. The actual cost of the day's shoot – crew, equipment hire, tape stock, meals, transport etc – was about £1,500.

To sum up, what I've described may seem rather haphazard and unsystematic, but I feel it gets nearer to the truth than many more organised, pre-planned documentaries. It also presents more opportunities for surprises. Following a professional around a site for a day, filming him doing his job, persuading him that you don't want him to do anything special – walk through his office door three times until the cameraman gets it right, for example – can produce material that is fascinating and entertaining for the viewer, and also illuminating about his task as he goes about his job. Such sequences of film can hopefully hold some recognisable truth about the business of designing and constructing buildings. Δ

To change life, however, we must first change space.[1]

Patrick Keiller interviewed by Joe Kerr

Joe Kerr Your journey from architecture to film places you in a particularly advantageous position from which to comment on the relationship between the two. What was it in particular that film-making offered to you – in terms of ideas or image-making for instance – that architecture had failed to deliver?

Patrick Keiller The film-making grew out of attempts to document various examples of built structures in which I detected architectural qualities, characteristics that were perhaps not intended by their builders. I didn't set out to make films, merely to collect these found buildings, which were initially documented as colour slides. The films evolved out of an idea that it was necessary, or at any rate possible, to say something about these images. Fairly early on in this process I discovered that there was a tradition of interest in found buildings – beyond that of architects looking for precedents – especially among artists who considered themselves to be, or were admired by, Surrealists. At about this time, I found the passage in Raoul Vaneigem's *The Revolution of Everyday Life*, which is quoted in the opening sequence of *Robinson in Space*:

Although I can always see how beautiful anything could be if only I could change it, in practically every case there is nothing I can

really do. Everything is changed into something else in my imagination, then the dead weight of things changes it back into what it was in the first place. A bridge between imagination and reality must be built.[2]

The spaces of everyday life are transformed in various ways; as a result of changes in economic, social and hence spatial relationships, by new technologies and so on. In the context of landscape and built structures one can distinguish between actual physical alteration – that is, the production of new architecture – and the subjective transformation of already existing space (what Lefebvre identifies as representational space[3]), which is a phenomenon more usually characteristic of literature and visual art, in particular photography and film, but which often has some reflexive impact on the physical environment.

At a lecture you gave a few years ago at the Royal Institute of British Architects (RIBA) I clearly remember you saying you were unconvinced that film was the best medium for representing architecture, as most people assume it to be. One of your arguments concerned the amount of information still photographs were capable of holding in contrast to film, another was about the ways in which film only gave the pretence of being experiential – it cannot depict the areas behind you and out of your vision, which are important in the way we 'sense' space. Could you elaborate on your misgivings about filming architecture? You also suggested that perhaps abstract, animated film might

Opposite
Robinson in Space
(BFI Stills)

Above
London
(BFI Stills)

be better able to represent architectural qualities on film. Would you still say that?

Well – I don't know what people assume, but the fact is that after more than 100 years of cinema, hardly anyone ever makes a film with the sole purpose of representing architecture, and one must wonder why this is. Two very obvious reasons suggest themselves: first of all, making films is generally very expensive and time consuming (not much less so than building buildings) and secondly, buildings don't move very much.

There is obviously an enormous amount of architecture represented in films and other moving pictures, but anyone who thinks that *The Third Man* was produced in order to represent Vienna, or that *Tomb Raider III* was produced in order to represent Venice is, I would suggest, in danger of missing the point, which is not that film is or isn't an effective way of representing space, but that it transforms it. Films don't represent experience of architecture, they reconstruct it.

To be more specific to your question, I often point out two things: firstly, that as a photographic medium cine film is a rather rudimentary way of representing architecture compared to the professional standard of large-format architectural photography. Secondly, and much more crucially, film space and actual space are very different. A film's audience certainly might hear what is offscreen, but visually film space is an assembly of discontinuous two-dimensional fragments, whereas actual space is a three-dimensional continuity.

The history of architectural photography is characterised by images in which space is most often represented as 'felt volume', in perspective, in a way that even a major avant-garde figure like Moholy-Nagy wasn't able to challenge to any great extent, at least

in his films of already existing architecture. It is very interesting to compare his pre-Vertov film proposal *Dynamic of the Metropolis* (1921–22), with the films that he actually managed to make – I'm thinking here of the city films like *Marseille Vieux Port*, rather than *Lichtspiel: Schwarz-Weiss-Grau*, which was a study of his light-space modulator, and is a definitive Modernist work.

So let me get this clear: you are claiming that photography, which has often been represented as a quintessentially modern practice, has struggled to frame architecture with a Modernist viewpoint?

Photography is an invention of the mid-19th century, isn't it? Architectural photography, if one can distinguish it as such – the photography of Atget, Bernd and Hilla Becher, Thomas Struth, Andreas Gursky, for example – generally represents space by creating an illusion of depth in a two-dimensional image. It's often suggested that this illusion of depth is produced most successfully in high contrast, high resolution, monochrome images, and it appears there may be some more or less credible neurological basis for this.

Now obviously, in the cinema – with montage and camera movement – there is a little more going on. But if one goes along with the notion of the primacy of the shot – as in practice I do, since I don't shoot from a script – the most striking architectural images are generally those that represent space in a way that I have always identified with what Reyner Banham described as 'the Lippsian idea of space, as felt volume, which is the sense it has in the writings of eg Muthesius',[4] rather than the 'later concept of space as a three-dimensional continuum, capable of metrical subdivision, without sacrifice of its continuity".[5] This is certainly the case, if only as a result of the proscenium frames of the camera's gate and the screen, which are fairly difficult to avoid, despite the efforts of many generations of avant-garde film-makers.

Cinema is essentially an invention of the era of the steam locomotive and the sewing machine, both of which pre-date Modernist architecture, though not the modern era. If one perseveres, it isn't too difficult to make photographs or images in films in which space is very effectively represented. But the space in the photograph or the film doesn't usually have an awful lot in common with the actual space that was in front of the camera, because of the overwhelming importance of the rectangular frame of the image, the narrow limits of the camera's field of view and so on. This misrepresentation of architecture by photography has been quite widely explored now, but the possibility for misrepresenting architecture in the cinema is even more inviting: it is one of the most enduring and attractive characteristics of the medium – indeed, in a way it's the whole point of the medium. As early as 1917, Kuleshov was writing about the construction of fictional architecture and geography by cutting together images of entirely discrete spaces, some of them thousands of miles apart. Such 'misrepresentation' is irrelevant unless one is trying to represent something intrinsic to the space in front of the camera, when it becomes a real problem. This is why it's so difficult to make documentary films about architecture. Some people say that it isn't even worth trying, but those who say this are, in my experience, quick to contrast this assertion with the importance of (fictional) architectural space in feature films etc. Again, the question isn't whether film is a medium for representing architectural space, but whether film space might or might not have anything to offer architecture that actually exists.

A number of contemporary architects have sought to extract new ideas or forms from the spatiality of film. Would you recognise film as a valid source for creating real spaces, or would you see that as a misguided project? Inversely, is there any way in which architecture can usefully inform the spatiality of film?

I'd recognise almost anything as a valid source for creating new spaces, but with film I do have trouble following the train of thought. This probably doesn't matter unless one finds the spaces lacking in some way, which in the examples I'm aware of I don't think I do, though I only know them from photographs.

Nonetheless, I can't help feeling that this train of thought doesn't always have that much to do with the results. For example, as far as I understand it, there is an idea around that some notion of montage can be introduced into architecture. In films, or at least in the kinds of films that most architects seem to watch, montage is usually employed to produce an illusion of spatiotemporal continuity from fragments that are actually discontinuous. Architects seem to be interested in montage as a means of fragmenting the spatiotemporal continuity of architectural space;

Below
Robinson in Space
(BFI Stills)

Opposite
London
(BFI Stills)

in other words, architects are trying to achieve the opposite result to that sought by film-makers. Isn't this another of those many cases in art where people are found not to be doing what they said they were doing, or what other people thought they had said they were doing, but what they did was OK, so it doesn't matter? To put this another way, I suspect that the film–architecture analogy is being used very selectively.

In my experience, what architects really like about cinema is that it can determine how architecture is experienced. Film is a kind of heightened awareness, and the representation of architecture in the cinema is, at its best, euphoric in a way that experience in everyday life only rarely is. Something of this seems to be getting back into actual built architecture, in the preference for certain kinds of surfaces and so on – rust, louvres, framing structures of all kinds – but this doesn't seem to be part of the polemic for 'cinematic' space.

I'm not sure what you mean by 'architecture informing the spatiality of cinema'. Architecture, or at least decor, has always been one of cinema's essentials, but it has always struck me that it's possible to create film space that is both extensive and euphoric from actual space that is humdrum, banal or even downright unpleasant. In any case, as I've said, the spatiality of cinema is put together rather differently from that of architecture, and the camera seems to be a rather old-fashioned way of approaching some more recent formulations of architectural space.

I don't know what new architecture and new cinema have to offer each other. No doubt there are all sorts of poetic possibilities, but at the moment the most obvious thing they have in common is that they're both increasingly difficult to realise. However, I've recently been watching archive television footage of

Constant's *New Babylon* models from the early 1960s, and it's very striking how much easier it is to see the architecture when it's been made into a film.

To what extent do you feel your own films, most obviously *London* (1994) and *Robinson in Space* (1997), are concerned with investigating architecture, or throw light on matters that concern architecture? In other words, to what extent does architecture remain a concern in your work? Have you any ambitions to develop further these ideas about the relationship of architecture and film in your own film-making?

I think you have to distinguish between architecture as the activity of designing built structures and architecture as the general phenomenon of built space, as experience. Obviously, these are films about the phenomenon of architecture; they have an awareness, a certain way of looking at it. They offer subjective transformations of already existing spaces, sometimes rather neglected spaces, which attempt to show 'how beautiful anything could be if only ...', and they offer the viewer a collective, shared experience of sights or spaces that are conventionally experienced in isolation; so they can be taken as a polemic for a kind of architectural experience, though it's not a new polemic. *London* set out to be both a critique and a reimagination of its subject.

In *Robinson in Space* I wanted to address the question of production. In the history of Modernism, a radical subjectivity of artists and writers to some already existing modernity often preceded the conscious application of these insights to design and production.

It's not so much that these films have something to offer architecture, as that they pick up ideas that are already familiar in architecture and put them in a wider cultural context. Recently, I've been making a television documentary about some aspects of house production. To some extent, this explores a particular approach to architectural design. It deals with architecture as a practice at least as much as a phenomenon, but it's also the least cinematic of the films I've made, and it has exposed an increasing tension between the subject of the films and their position in some kind of film culture – not to mention the problems of working exclusively for television. Up to now, I've tried to avoid the more depressing aspects of present-day film-making by claiming some residual allegiance to art, or architecture, or geography, or film history, or international Modernism or anything else I can think of. It seems to be increasingly difficult to make credible cinema, but in the end I think I shall have to try to confront the problem again, if it isn't too late. ∆

This interview took place in August 1999.

Footnotes
1. See Henri Lefebvre, *The Production of Space*, translated by Donald Nicholson-Smith, Blackwell, Oxford, 1991, p 190
2. The passage is from 'Radical Subjectivity', Section 3 of Chapter 23 of Raoul Vaneigem's *Traité de savoir-vivre l'usage des jeunes générations*, known in English as *The Revolution of Everyday Life*. This translation is by Christopher Gray, editor of *Leaving the Twentieth Century*, Free Fall Publications (London), 1974, p 138 in which Chapter 23 appears as 'Self-Realisation, Communication and Participation'.
3. *The Production of Space*, Lefebvre, p 39.
4. *Theory & Design in the First Machine Age*, Reyner Banham, Architectural Press (London), 1960, p 67.
5. Ibid.

James Bond, Stanley Kubrick, Captain Kirk and George Lucas

Therapeutic

The current aesthetic obsession with all things retro may give rise to criticism for its lack of progressiveness, but Bob Fear celebrates this movement by investigating one of the main sources of its inspiration – the Bond movie. He talks to Oscar winning production designer Peter Lamont on the set of *The World Is Not Enough* and looks at the genre-defining design ethics of his predecessor – the legendary Ken Adam – who shaped the 'Bond look' from *Dr No* to *Moonraker*. Fear then showcases new works by diverse architects Nicholas Grimshaw, Matthew Priestman, Wells Mackereth, Chetwood Associates and Anton Markus Pasing. These display influences from the science-fiction aesthetics of the Bond movies, *Dr Strangelove, 2001: A Space Odyssey, Star Trek* and *Star Wars*, all films designed over 20 years ago yet still informing today's architecture.

Visions

The continuing trend for all things retro stems from a fascination with 1960s Space-Age chic. With the space race to the stars on between the USA and USSR, the decade saw a new design aesthetic emerge, reflecting this new age of technological advancement. Sci-fi and fantasy films brought high technology within reach, forecasting how our lives might change within a few years.

The visionary talents of Oscar-winning production designer Ken Adam made real the possibilities of High-Tech , well before architects and interior designers were able to realise its potential. Adam influenced a whole generation by inventing the so-called 'Bond look'; his futuristic film sets have now become a reality – ironically, in homage to his work. Designers, such as Norman Foster, Nicholas Grimshaw, Jean Nouvel and Future Systems seem to be looking to the past – to the aesthetics of Bond, Stanley Kubrick's *2001: A Space Odyssey* (1968) and even the Gerry Anderson television series such as Thunderbirds to find their inspiration for the future. To complete the circle, the directors and designers of the new James Bond films are using modern, High-Tech architecture within their locations; as if the daring, dashing spy finally has a 'real' home in the new millennium to accommodate his jetsetting life style.

> (*The Spy Who Loved Me*) cost $13 million, lasts for two hours and five minutes, and the star of the show, yet again, is not Roger Moore. It is the designer Ken Adam.
> —Tim Radford, *Guardian*, 1977.

Bond Chic

The Bond look took off with *Goldfinger*. This was the first film to allow Ken Adam, who designed most of the Bond films from *Dr No* in 1962 to *Moonraker* in 1979, to explore his true potential. After the relative realism of *From Russia With Love*, Adam was free to indulge his visions of fantasy architecture already explored in Kubrick's *Dr Strangelove* of the same year and, thanks to it's increasing budget, to heighten the aesthetic appeal of the series. Adam had started out in theatre design, but found the straight representation behind the proscenium arch far too restricting. He preferred fantasy film, which provided a 'therapy for the mind' that gave free rein to his imagination, unravelling thoughts and ideas otherwise impossible to realise. The main challenge for each Bond film, Adam recalls, was having to provide a bigger, better, different lair for each successive villain. He accommodates Auric

Goldfinger in a Modernist Baltimore ranch. The sweeping lines, graceful curves and large, plain surfaces typify Adam's favoured interior decor – emphasising the affluence and grandeur essential to any worthy Bond baddie.

However, the plush surfaces use the Minimalist's trick of hiding the inner machinations of the built environment. The now clichéd device of bookcases, paintings and tables silently and effortlessly sweeping aside or overturning to reveal banks of flashing lights, computer spools and monitor screens is employed. This key Bondism of hiding, then revealing, the High-Tech behind either the natural or the luxurious can

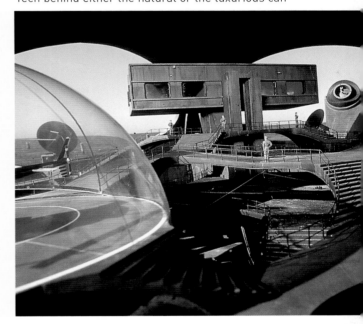

be found in most of the following films in the series, as the pretensions of the villain are discarded to reveal his true dastardly intentions. But good always triumphs, and Adam provides the heroes with equally ingenious undercover tactics to thwart the enemy.

In *You Only Live Twice* (Gilbert, 1967) Tiger Tanaka, the Japanese Secret Service's counterpart to our own M, has a hidden, subterranean base beneath a dark, Brutalist car park in downtown Tokyo. We only ever see it accessed through a concealed trap door, which gives way to a sleek, minimal, brightly lit, steel-clad network of corridors and spacious offices. M's modern, mobile headquarters in *The Man With the Golden Gun* are ensconced within the capsized wreck of the rusted *Queen Elizabeth* off Hong Kong bay and, in *The Spy Who Loved Me*, amongst the ancient monuments, statues and carvings of Karnak in Egypt.

However, in each of these films, the villain's lair wins the competition for clever camouflaging. In *The Man With the Golden Gun*, Adam locates the evil Scaramangar's High-Tech complex within the very rocks of the picturesque, idyllic Thai island of Khow-Ping-

Opposite
Nicholas Grimshaw and Partners' HAL 9000, Cemex global production and distribution centre, Mexico

Above right
The Spy Who Loved Me
(MGM/BFI Stills)

Khan near Phuket. In *You Only Live Twice*, Ernst Blofeld's SPECTRE rocket base is hidden beneath a volcano. Here, Adam takes the hidden High-Tech Bondism to its limits: the exterior shots of the breathtaking volcanic landscape were filmed on the island of Matsu, near Shanghai, whilst the interior was the largest studio film set so far built at Pinewood. It was constructed using:

200 miles of tubular steel; over 700 tons of structural steel; 200 tons of plasterwork; half a million tubular couplings (weighing more than the combined tonnage of 1,100 family cars); 8,000 railway sleepers for the monorail (at a cost of 16/9 each) and more than 250,000 square yards of canvas. The result of 379 conceptual drawings realised by 250 plasterers, riggers, painters and carpenters working seven days a week.[1]

But Adam's desire for extreme scale and grandeur outdid this feat 10 years later. No existing studio space was large enough to accommodate his vision of how Karl Stromberg's aquatic lair, Atlantis, in *The Spy Who Loved Me* should look. Costing $1 million and constructed at Pinewood – it was the largest sound stage in the world, providing a floor space of 374 by 160 feet and a height of 53 feet. The result is a realisation of a fantasy palace in the sea (off the coast of Sardinia) with a futuristic, sweeping geometry of steel walls and walkways.

The key to the success of the fantasy technology in the Bond films is its firm grounding in reality. For example. at a time when breakthroughs were being made in laser technology, *Goldfinger* featured the very first onscreen use of a laser beam – admittedly overlaid with an optical effect created by an oxyacetalene torch to increase its punch.[2] This 'reality' culminated in Ken Adam's last Bond picture: 1979's *Moonraker* (Gilbert). Again, the villain's lair is an attempt to outdo all of its predecessors, and this time it is hidden in outer space. Adam and his art director, Peter Lamont, worked with NASA to develop their designs for Hugo Drax's space station and realise a legitimate vision of how such an environment would be. The three-tiered set was constructed at the Epinay and Ballincourt Studios north of Paris and became the largest ever built in France, costing £250,000 and using 220 technicians, 100 tons of metal, 2 tons of nails and 10,000 feet of wood.[3] As Peter Lamont recalls, the premiere of *Moonraker* was intended to coincide with the latest NASA space-shuttle launch. Inevitably, NASA's blastoff was delayed, but *Moonraker* succeeded where practicality-bound reality lagged behind.

Opposite top
Goldfinger (MGM/BFI Stills)

Opposite bottom right
Pinewood Studios during
the construction of the set
for *You Only Live Twice*
(MGM/BFI Stills)

Opposite bottom left
You Only Live Twice
(MGM/BFI Stills)

Above and far right
Moonraker
(MGM/BFI Stills)

Right
You Only Live Twice
(MGM/BFI Stills)

Bond Tech

Peter Lamont is the production designer on the 19th Bond film – *The World Is Not Enough* (Michael Apted) – which premiered in London in November 1999. He began his film art training on the early Bond pictures under Ken Adam and has now designed all of the Bonds since *Octopussy* (John Glen) in 1983. He was also production designer on the James Cameron epics *Aliens* (1986), *True Lies* (1994) and *Titanic* (1997), for which he won an Oscar.

Lamont describes his design approach as being 'as realistic as possible', learning from Adam – who famously received concerned enquiries about how he managed to shoot inside Fort Knox for *Goldfinger*. (The only giveaway that Adam had imagined these interiors was that the gold was stacked as far and high as the eye could see, when in reality, it cannot be stacked higher than 2 feet). A similar challenge met Lamont when designing the office for M and Miss Moneypenny for the Pierce Brosnan films. He insisted that they had to be seen to fit realistically into the MI6 offices on the south bank of the Thames, particularly as the exterior is featured in the films. 'My starting point was to imagine where the senior official's offices may be from the placing of the exterior windows. I then designed oak-panelled interiors accordingly.' Lamont prefers to use all the real materials suggested by the set designs in order to convey the true texture and quality under studio lighting. He is therefore proud of his use of real oak columns for the rotundas on the set of the Titanic, which Leonardo DiCaprio hides behinds in close-up – 'ply panels just become repetitive!'

Lamont's desire for realism and the use of existing architecture is apparent throughout *The World Is Not Enough*. Oil City in Baku is featured, for example, and the nuclear test facility in Kazakhstan is based on outlets in the Eurotunnel. For the scenes set on the rooftops of Elektra King's headquarters, Lamont used the Motorola manufacturing facility in Swindon, which he discovered whilst driving along the M4: 'I was instantly attracted to its gleaming, High-Tech apparel and thought it the ideal Bond location.'

Director Michael Apted was keen to be the first to use the Millennium Dome in a film, so Lamont and his team had to finish off landscaping a section of the surrounding grounds to give the Greenwich landmark a completed appearance, eight months before its New Year grand opening. Apted says of his desire to use Frank Gehry's Guggenheim Museum in Bilbao: 'It's beautiful, it's exotic, it's a good Bond location and it's also contemporary. This is the Bond film for the millennium and this is the building for the millennium.'

Lamont describes how he works on his designs: 'At each stage, I take care to see how the set works photographically. I build up small-scale cardboard models from plans and elevations and then use a 'lipstick' camera, hooked up to a video monitor, which in turn is hooked up to a printer. As the tiny camera tracks through certain shots the director may want to use, I click on key frames, which are then printed out to form a storyboard of that scene.' He constructed cardboard models of all the major set pieces in *The World Is Not Enough*, including the Millennium Dome and the MI6 building. This enables a shooting script to be meticulously planned, long before location work takes place, thus ensuring the shoot is as organised and efficient as possible – particularly important when filming in the middle of central London, which can be fraught with logistical problems.

For the industrial, High-Tech interior sets of the submarine, the Bond crew returned to Pinewood for the first time in ten years. They again used the massive water-tank facility, built for the submarine-dock interior of the Liparus supertanker in *The Spy Who Loved Me*. For *The World Is Not Enough*, a whole section of the submarine interior was built so that it could be suspended over the water tank and then lowered into it on cue as the upturned submarine filled with water.

As for the future of Bond, Lamont is adamant that the series cannot go back to the old-style aesthetic: 'It has to be steered gently in a new direction' – which for the moment is based firmly in realism, drawing inspiration from existing works of architecture. Architects throughout the world whose dream it is that one of their projects may be used as a location in a future Bond film may be lucky.

Bond Living

Somewhere on the edge of a scorching, hostile desert, a small blank structure is etched into a sandy embankment. As your chauffeur-driven car pulls up, the unattended door slides open, revealing a dark, raked cutting; a causeway demarcated by lamps. This leads to the glistening silver spectacle beyond – an oasis of luxury apartments, bars, restaurants, sports facilities, swimming pools and landscaped gardens. This three-storey, curved roof structure is mirrored by a sister building, which, on stilt supports, stands proudly offshore in the azure sea, accessible by service tunnel, speedboat or helicopter.

Matthew Priestman Architects have proposed a luxury hotel fit for an undercover liaison between 007 and a corrupt, multimillionaire oil baron. Ken Adam couldn't have imagined it better. This Bond-like High-Tech complex reflects the aquatic theme of Stromberg's Atlantis and has even been likened to Tracey Island. It is a soon-to-be-realised fantasy is resplendent in its unashamed display of affluence, sitting amidst the impenetrable heat of the harsh Arabian desert. Its roof is laced with solar-powered diachronic-cell networks to maintain an ice-cool internal temperature. Regular elevator towers act as wind tunnels, and the rear of the building is screened with a stretched surface of brise-soleil, with parking bays beneath.

The entrance is a triple-height, cavernous void, dominated by a circular glass diving pool, which rises through the roof. Marble floors extend effortlessly through to the landscaped interior beyond, which consists of overlapping terraces with rock pools, fountains, waterfalls and exotic planting. Curved dividing walls separate eating, playing and shaded areas.

Priestman's team are pandering to that ache that craves a life as part of a glamorous, jetsetting, high-budget Bond film, where the technological wizardry is solid reality, a small part of paradise for the lucky few hiding amongst the never-ending sand dunes. Just beware of the hidden trap doors over those shark-infested waters.

Strange Loft

Ken Adam proudly recalls how, during a recent industry tribute to the late Stanley Kubrick, Steven Spielberg told him his design of the war room in *Dr Strangelove* was his favourite ever set design. High commendation indeed, but Adam's other favourite anecdote relays how – on achieving his Presidential post at the White House – Ronald Reagan asked his aides when he could see the war room portrayed in the Kubrick classic! This is a perfect example of how real the fictional film world is to the impressionable viewer; or at least, an example of how much we wish it were reality. Some of us, it seems, go to great lengths to snatch a piece of that celluloid world and drag it into our everyday lives. Beyond the notion of visiting larger-than-life, film-studio theme parks that re-create our favourite blockbuster moments, is the Postmodern notion of turning our homes into our favourite film set.

Wells Mackereth, a young architectural practice based in the heart of London's Soho, have a diverse portfolio of work including houses and apartments for a range of clients with unusual tastes. Their approach to each project is not preconditioned by a house style, but firmly based on a belief in the fluidity of space and careful attention to detail, both of which are essential to their projects. Whilst clearly rooted in Modernism, their work has a more catholic approach, combining unlikely materials and textures to create intriguing spaces for a modern way of life. Their designs put a contemporary spin on Le Corbusier's idea of the house as a 'machine for living'.

'During the initial briefing stages of a project, clients often refer to a specific moment in a movie to describe their fantasy life style. It's as if Bond took Modernism and made it accessible, groovy and decadent – everyone wants a drop-down, foldaway, slide-out, back-lit, built-in something or other in their new home', says Sally Mackereth. When a young director of commercials recently commissioned Wells Mackereth, they set about designing less of a traditional home and more of a fantasy lair.

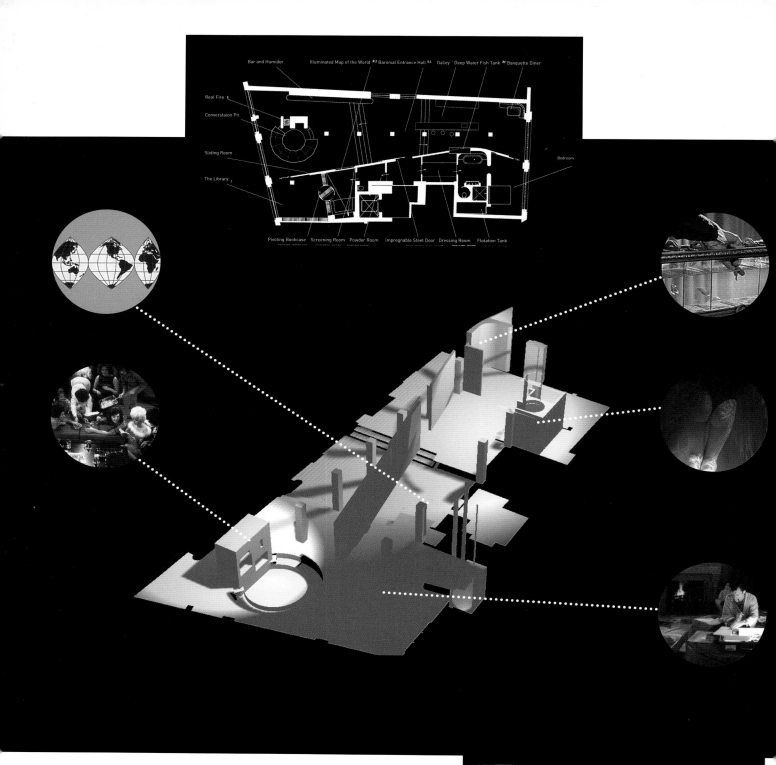

Bar and Humidor   Illuminated Map of the World   Baronial Entrance Hall   Galley   Deep Water Fish Tank   Banquette Diner

Real Fire

Conversation Pit

Sliding Room

The Library

Bedroom

Pivoting Bookcase   Screening Room   Powder Room   Impregnable Steel Door   Dressing Room   Flotation Tank

Key elements in this loft apartment include a
sunken conversation pit with stone-clad open
fireplace and a pivoting door concealed in a wall
of books leading to a private screening room.
A section of the curved rosewood wall draws
across to reveal a floor-to-ceiling illuminated
map of the world; a large tropical-fish tank
built into the wall adjacent to the bath gives
the bather a unique underwater Jacques
Cousteau bathtime experience.

The resident of this loft is then free to live
out his ideological life style, somewhere between
the worlds of Auric Goldfinger and Hugh Heffner,
via the imagination of Ken Adam.

HAL Now

HAL 9000 is the ultimate realisation of the fusion between film fantasy and architectural reality. This computer centre unashamedly takes its name and its look from Kubrick's seminal sci-fi flick *2001: A Space Odyssey*. Designing for Cemex, one of the foremost producers of cement in Mexico, Nicholas Grimshaw and Partners have drawn inspiration from the concept and design of Arthur C Clarke's HAL 9000 computer intelligence, whose omnipotence is felt at every turn in the Discovery One spacecraft.

The brief asked for a futuristic interior – so, irony intact, it was back to Tony Masters, Harry Lange and Ernest Archer's production designs from 1967 for a template from which to draw. Although Grimshaw's is not a spacecraft interior it seems that, as with Ken Adam, Masters, Lange and Archer's prophecies have become self-fulfilling. It's nearly Clarke's landmark, year of 2001, and as far as we know we haven't made contact, but HAL 'lives and breathes' in waiting, under the sweltering heat of the Monterey sun.

HAL on Earth is a one-storey-high white box with only a few office windows. Like its fictional forebear, its sentient qualities are enhanced by its ability to operate and control – in this case Cemex's global production and distribution –

24 hours a day, 365 days a year, overseen by the 'eye' of the operation: the constantly manned control desk, which is on a raised elliptical platform overlooking the computer room. If an unforeseen problem should occur and human presence is required amidst the sterile calm of the computer area, you are granted access through movement-sensitive glass doors, which slide aside. Your presence then activates human-friendly lighting, which automatically switches off once you are no longer detectable, returning HAL to its quiet state of grace.

Ever security conscious, HAL even appears to scan its visitors as they enter. Recessed red gobos in the ceiling illuminate the stainless steel 'airlock' before a second set of doors beyond the entrance slides open. Once inside, the blue-tinted glass lenses in the floor convey an 'ice house' atmosphere which reflects the heavily controlled environment, protecting all inside from the exterior temperature. Even when you begin to suffer from computer fatigue, HAL provides a white, tensioned sail-wall suspended from concrete beams. The wall can be used as a projection screen for Cemex-friendly presentations to clients as well as a focal point for the control-desk operators. HAL likes to keep its inhabitants happy. This is no place for paranoid conspiracy theorists, but a brilliant retrospective tribute to a thirty year old concept, providing its inhabitants with the comfort and familiarity of an environment that ironically affirms how they thought things should be looking in 2001.

Opposite top
Wells Mackereth's loft apartment for a film director

Opposite bottom
Dr Strangelove (Columbia Tristar/BFI Stills)

Above left
Nicholas Grimshaw and Partners' HAL 9000, Cemex global production and distribution centre, Mexico.

Above right
2001: A Space Odyssey (Warner Brothers/The Ronald Grant Archive).

Above
Chetwood Associates'
Kevlavik Airport, Iceland

Opposite
Natwalk
Anton Markus Pasing

Footnotes
1. *Kiss Kiss Bang Bang!*
Alan Barnes & Marcus
Hearn, Batsford, 1997, UK.
2. Ibid.
3. Ibid.

Ice Trek

Paul Grayshon, the project architect for Chetwood Associates, maintains that the as yet unbuilt design for an expansion of the existing airport at Kevlavik near Reykjavik in Iceland, was never meant to be seen as a homage to sci-fi film aesthetics. Perhaps this reflects how the iconic imagery of *Star Trek*'s Starship Enterprise is ingrained in our subconscious.

It's as if Captain Kirk has temporarily lost control of the Enterprise under threat of Klingon attack, and hastily set down in the alien landscape of a hostile volcanic moor, punctuated by hot springs spurting vapour into the atmosphere. In all directions, each horizon holds a contrasting view – mountain, sea or glacier. Daylight comes and goes in a few short hours, the only other light coming from the awe-inspiring spectral Aurora Borealis. Anyone stopping over here between Europe and the USA, would be likely to think they had landed on an alien planet – but would perhaps feel somehow at home with the strange familiarity of the architecture.

Park Wars

Thanks to constant exposure to sci-fi films from an early age, we have a natural faith in High-Tech. Anton Markus Pasing takes advantage of this in his fairytale Natwalk project. In order convincingly to convey the notion of machines that come to life and stalk our cities, Pasing uses parts of the All Terrain Armoured Transports (AT-ATs) from *The Empire Strikes Back* (Irvin Kershner, 1980) in his designs for an ecologically sound solution to the dominance of urbanity. His wish is to activate patterns of experience that already exist in our mind in order to engage our sympathy for his ethically minded machines.

Blurring the borders between fantasy and reality, Pasing asks us to forget Central Park, and instead let ourselves be swept up from the grey, concrete, overcrowded, polluted streets by these monolithic technological creatures who provide a green haven on their familiar shoulders. He taps into the part of our imaginations that would dearly love to live with George Lucas-style technology, and be taken by X-Wings to the orange skies over a sprawling Art Deco metropolis – flying to the safety of a secret hide-out in the green rainforests of an orbiting moon. Δ⃝

Biographies

△D Architecture + Film II

Rachel Armstrong is the editor of *Sci Fi Aesthetics* and *Space Architecture* published by Wiley-Academy. She is also a television presenter, lecturer at The Bartlett School of Architecture, a multimedia producer and medical doctor specialising in the evolution of humankind through 'unnatural interventions'. She also has a forthcoming fiction book for Serpents Tail *A Gray's Anatomy*.

Jonathan Bell is a writer and freelance journalist. After studying Illustration and Design History, he spent four years working for a London firm of architects. He is currently preparing *The Transformable House* issue of △D for publication.

Iain Borden is Director of Architectural History and Theory at The Bartlett, University College London, where he is Reader in Architecture and Urban Culture. He is co-editor of *Architecture and the Sites of History* (1995), *Strangely Familiar* (1996), *Gender Space Architecture* (1999), *The Unknown City* (2000), *The City Cultures Reader* (2000), and *InterSections* (2000). He is the author of *Architecture in Motion: Skateboarding and Urban Experience*, and, with Jane Rendell, of *DoubleDecker: Architecture through History, Politics and Poetics*, (both forthcoming).

Karin Damrau graduated in 1995 from FHT, Stuttgart, later studying in Bordeaux and Zurich. She then worked as an architect in Hamburg for two years before receiving a grant from the German Academic Exchange Service to study for a Master's Degree at The Bartlett School of Architecture, University College London, from which she graduated with distinction in 1998. Since 1999 she has been a teaching assistant at the Technical University of Aachen (RWTH), Department of Architectural Design and Building Typology, with Professor Klaus Kada.

Claudia Dillmann studied German literature, film sciences and art history at Frankfurt/Main after an education in journalism. She went on to assist in setting up the German Film Museum where she became Deputy Director from 1992 to 1997.She has produced numerous exhibitions and published several works on German film. Claudia is now the director of the Deutsches Filminstitut – DIF and undertakes teaching assignments on film architecture and social history of film at Frankfurt University.

Stephanie Ellis lives in San Francisco and teaches visual culture at the San Francisco Art Institute and the California College of Arts and Crafts.

Bob Fear graduated in Drama & Media from the University of London before helping to set up the London Film Commission, after which he went on to work in location management in films. He is currently a freelance journalist and is editor of the Cyberspace pages of the forthcoming △D website.

Murray Grigor, whose latest film on Alexander 'Greek' Thomson *Nineveh on the Clyde*, is obsessed with bringing architecture to a new audience and has just become the first film-maker to be made an honorary fellow of the RIBA. His many award winners include *Mackintosh*, 1968; *Frank Lloyd Wright*, 1981; and *Carlo Scarpa*, 1996.

Eric Hanson is a designer specialising in the creation of digital environments for film. His architectural experience includes The Callison Partnership and Gensler, and his film credits include a 70mm film, *Mars Odyssey*, Luc Besson's *The Fifth Element*, and Walt Disney's feature animations *Atlantis*, and *Fantasia 2000*. Eric recently completed work at Dream Quest Images for Bicentennial Man. Eric holds a degree in Architecture from the University of Texas at Austin.

Edwin Heathcote is an architect and writer living and working in London. He writes on architecture for the *Financial Times* and has written several books for Wiley-Academy: *Imre Makovecz*, *Monument Builders* and *Bank Builders*. He is currently writing *Cinema Builders*, due to be published later this year.

Joe Kerr is Senior Tutor in Historical and Critical Studies at the Royal College of Art, London. A founding member of Strangely Familiar, he is co-editor of *Strangely Familiar: Narratives of Architecture in the City* (1996) and *The Unknown City: Contesting Architecture and Social Space* (2000). He is currently writing *The Special Relationship: the Influence of America on British Architecture since 1945* with Murray Fraser.

Peter Lyssiotis is a photo monteur, film-maker and writer. He is currently artist-in-residence at the Centre for Design, RMIT University, Melbourne, Australia. He has published numerous small press books including *Journey of a Wise Electron and Other Stories* (1984), *Three Cheers for Civilisation* (1986) and *The Harbour Breathes* (with Anna Couani) (1988). His photographs and limited edition artist's books include *The Harmed Circle* (1992), *Feather & Prey* (1997) and *The Look of Love* (with Scott McQuire) (1998). His film *The Occupant* (1985) and video *Thug* (1997) (with Christos Tsiolkas and Spiros Economopoulos) have been widely screened.

Scott McQuire is an Australian Postdoctoral Research Fellow at the School of Social Inquiry, Deakin University, Australia. He is the author of *Visions of Modernity: Representation, Memory, Time and Space in the Age of the Camera* (Sage, London, 1998) and is currently researching the intercations between architecture and mass media.

Martin Price teaches Film and Media Studies at Stratford-Upon-Avon College. He is also a research student at Loughborough University and is currently working on his Doctoral thesis on cinematic representations of the city.

Heather Puttock is a graduate of the MA programme at the British Film Institute. She is currently a freelance journalist working at *The Guardian's* FilmUnlimited website.

Karl Sabbagh was educated at King's College, Cambridge. He joined the BBC in 1965 as a science producer and between 1965 and 1978 worked on a range of documentary programmes, including *Horizon*, *Controversy*, *Inside Medicine*, *The Changing Face of Medicine*, *A Question of Mirrors* and *The Body in Question*. After leaving the BBC he made a wide range of documentary programmes for two independent companies which he set up – InCA and Skyscraper Productions. They include documentaries about anthropology, nuclear power, mathematics, alternative medicine, cosmology, airplane construction, Victorian London and Erik Satie. His most recent books include *Skyscraper*, *Twenty-First Century Jet*, *A Rum Affair* and, in press, *Power into Art*.

Hans Dieter Schaal studied architecture in Hannover and Stuttgart. He now works as a freelance artist, an architect, exhibition and stage designer and landscape architect. In the last ten years he has provided expansive installations for the broadest possible range of exhibition subjects, from *100 Years of Film* at the Stiftung Deutsche Kinemathek in Berlin to *City Building Culture in the 21st Century* at the Architecture Biennale in Venice. He is currently planning the new Berlin Film Museum. His publications include *In-Between: Exhibition Architecture* (Menges, 1999) and *Interior Spaces* (Ernst & John, 1995)

Katherine Shonfield studied sociology and worked as local authority planner before qualifying as an architect. She lectures in history and theory at South Bank University, is a weekly columnist on the *Architects Journal*, deputy editor of *The Journal of Architecture*, and is a member of the Royal Society of Arts' Art for Architecture Committee and the Architectural Association. She is a principal on the practice Shonfield and Williams and a consultant to Muf Architects.

Peter Pran

Few architects have made it their mission to produce cutting-edge designs for corporate and institutional clients. Soren Larson pays tribute to Peter Pran, who has been creating non-hierarchical, community-orientated structures within large commercial firms since graduating from Mies van der Rohe's Chicago-based office in the 1960s.

When Peter Pran – as part of the American and Norwegian architect team NBBJ-HUS-PKA – won the commission to design the huge Telenor Telecommunications Headquarters in Oslo, Norway, in 1998, it wasn't just another job for the veteran architect. For one thing, it was to be the first design in Europe by NBBJ, Pran's Seattle, Washington-based firm. Beyond that, it was the first time that he would be practising architecture in his home country, which he had left almost 40 years before to find his way in America. Pran was well aware of the ramifications.

'To win the competition was wonderful for the entire NBBJ-HUS-PKA architect team, and it was particularly emotional for me as an Norwegian-American, to work on my first project in Norway', he says. 'This is where I was born and lived half my life, the other half in America; I feel I belong to both countries. It is exhilarating for all of us to now see this project under construction'. The highly modernistic Telenor project is significant in another, less immediately obvious way. NBBJ is the second-largest architectural firm in the US; it works on huge corporate complexes, stadiums, and all manner of building types for high-powered clients – the majority of whom are not known as patrons of cutting-edge architecture. But Pran and the design teams are managing to produce experimental, complex designs while working within this challenging milieu. 'I do have a certain pride in that I am one of the persons bringing avant-garde architecture to the large firms', he says.

It hasn't necessarily been easy. Pran describes his striving to install leading-edge architecture at his former firm, Ellerbe Becket, as 'sometimes an uphill struggle'. But the partners at NBBJ, he says, are committed. This was a major reason many of his former colleagues at Ellerbe Becket have done the same thing. 'Many of us went to NBBJ because they had the most open minds', says Pran, who is quick to add that the architects decided to jump ship individually; there was no team strategy to do so.

Pran says 'NBBJ is committed to doing very good modern architecture. The principals and partners have very open minds – which is wonderful, considering that some large firms don't. The real key is to get an entire firm committed to the kind of ideals that perhaps a small group is pursuing, because then everyone becomes open to new ideas'.

Pran is well-rooted in the basic tenets of Modernism, and is keenly interested in introducing new forms to urban skylines. His designs are often asymmetrical, with curving forms that play off one another in a dynamic fashion. He also stresses social ideas such as being non-hierarchical and introducing open, egalitarian spaces to venues that were once rigidly bureaucratic. To further that aim, he pursues the notion of seemingly limitless space, with flowing forms that curve together with no clear beginning or ending. It is an obvious thought that he might have been better served in a boutique firm or by running his own practice. Nevertheless, Pran stresses that he feels 'very comfortable in a large firm where you have incredible resources and expertise. In a small firm you have to pay attention to the accounting, you have to go out and hustle and take care of every detail'.

NBBJ is now involved in many high quality architecture projects. In the firm's hometown of Seattle, NBBJ's Joey Myers, John Savo, Scott Wyatt, Scott Johnson, Louisa Chang and Pran are leading a group designing a headquarters for Vulcan Northwest, the asset management company owned by Paul Allen, the multibillionaire cofounder of Microsoft, who has become one of the most important architectural clients in America. NBBJ has designed a sculpted, irregular glass structure that respects its historic surroundings while adding a strikingly modernistic presence to the neighbourhood.

Across the Pacific, NBBJ won an international competition in 1997 to design the Seoul Dome, a multipurpose sports facility and entertainment centre that will host the World Cup in 2002. The complex will also include 2 million square feet of convention halls, restaurants, banquet facilities, cinemas and stores, and the architects – Dan Meis and Pran, design principals, together with lead designers Jonathan Ward and Joey Myers and a squadron of others in the Los Angeles NBBJ office– have strung the functions together into a single, flowing entity. 'The key to the solution for us was to make it truly mixed-use, with all the different functions interacting in one pulsating whole', says Pran. 'There are theatres that transform into exhibition space that transform into seating in the stadium, that again transform into entertainment walkways. It is one of the foremost designs we have done, because it didn't start with a shape, but with a programme that we reinterpreted and intertwined. The completed design has a feeling of endless space.'

Telenor Telecommunications Headquarters, Oslo

Vulcan Northwest Headquarters, Seattle, Washington

For Vulcan Northwest, NBBJ's Joey Myers, John Savo, Scott Johnson, Louisa Chang and Peter Pran are leading a group designing a striking sculptural building.

In 1998, NBBJ, allied with two Norwegian firms HUS and PKA, won the international competition to design the Telenor Telecommunications Headquarters in Oslo. The design team is led by Jan Storing, Bjorn Sorum, Jonathan Ward, Jin Ah Park, Annema Selstrom, Scott Wyatt and Peter Pran, and with Joey Myers during the competition.

Pran appears to be in his prime, with several ongoing projects around the world, from Scandinavia to Asia, but he finds it unimportant to mention his age. Still, it is clear that he has compiled a long list of essential experiences, starting with a mentorship with a master: two years after graduation from Oslo's Arkitekthoyskole, Pran departed for Chicago and ended up knocking on the office door of Ludwig Mies Van der Rohe, looking for work. Mies took him in. 'When I went over to Chicago I actually had no idea if I could work for him. The day I was hired, I had just a couple of bucks left', Pran smiles. 'So I took a big chance. And there were only about 18 to 20 people there. I was very lucky and it has been an enormous experience.'

Pran worked on the design and key details of the National Gallery in Berlin 1963-68 and toiled with Mies on the Chicago Federal Center and the Toronto Dominion Center. He also constructed several touchstone friendships in his early years in Chicago, including one with Phyllis Lambert, founder of the influential Canadian Center for Architecture. That relationship peaked recently when Pran, together with Joey Myers, Andrea Bettella, Jin Ah Park and Jonathan Ward, created a 10-foot-by-3-foot collage of their work in NBBJ and donated it to the centre. He also met his wife, Clevon – a black artist active in the civil rights movement – in Chicago and was with her until 1998, when she died after a long illness. Together with Phyllis, the collage was donated in memory of Clevon Pran.

Mies' firm was just an initial professional stop. Next came Skidmore, Owings & Merrill, where he stayed for seven years. He left that huge firm to join Schmidt, Garden & Erikson, which has since disbanded, and from there Pran ventured to the New York area, working for Grad Partnership and then for ten years at Ellerbe Becket as design principle in charge, before joining NBBJ on the West Coast. He's also been an adjunct or associate professor at 12 universities, his most recent stop being Cornell University, where he was team teaching with other designers from NBBJ during the fall 1999 semester. Along the way, he's stepped out of the master's shadow and found his own voice. 'One of the toughest things in my life was to free myself and find my own direction', Pran remembers. 'Many people that worked with Frank Lloyd Wright, Le Corbusier and Mies tended to stay in that direction. I'm proud that I found my own direction; it took me a number of years. My change came also from being an architecture professor. New ideas came from working and dialoguing with students, and it moved the thought process forward.'

Pran undertook a number of sizable projects at Ellerbe Becket, including three notable structures recently completed in the New York City metropolitan area: the interior of the headquarters of advertising agency Deloitte & Touche; the New York Psychiatric Institute in upper Manhattan; and a new academic complex at the State University of New York at Binghamton. The latter two are vintage Pran: curving,

asymmetrical shapes with ample amounts of glass and other connections with the community. The Institute's shape is defined by a research wing to the north and a patient's wing to the south, while a soaring, six-storey atrium unifies the wings and acts as the focal point of circulation. The curving, western facade reflects the traffic of the nearby West Side Highway and unites the two programmatic masses. Neighbourhood views were maintained and pedestrian bridges built for easy access. At Binghamton, the new facilities operate as a gateway to the campus and gives a modern edge to the school. The two curved, glass structures break the campus' existing grid to create an open expression of movement.

Back in Oslo, NBBJ is now working with the two Norwegian architecture firms, HUS and PKA, on the complex for Telenor. In order to cope with the size of the project – the headquarters, at 2 million square feet, will be the largest office building in Norway – the three firms together have set up an architect office in Oslo, where Pran has been spending time. The scenic site overlooks the Oslofjord and is the former site of the Oslo International Airport, which has moved to a new location. The design encompasses offices, boulevards, and public pavilions, and will house at least 6,000 employees.

NBBJ-HUS-PKA's design team – led by Jan Storing, Bjorn Sorum, Jonathan Ward, Jin Ah Park, Annema Selstrom, Scott Wyatt, Joey Myers and Pran – worked on a module, requested by the client, of 30 people per office unit. The workstations and meeting rooms emphasise flexibility and openness. To harmonise with the low-lying, waterfront site, the complex is set on the axis of the airport runway, and at the centre, two huge glass wings – one bent, one curved – run alongside one another toward the fjord. The offices fan out to the sides of these central wings, which will serve as circulation boulevards for workers and visitors. Pran says the glass boulevards will create a feeling of free movement and democracy among the staff, because the spaces invite communication and interactivity.

Telenor is a top priority at the moment, but it is also a major step for NBBJ toward a more global mindset. 'As a major leading design firm you have to be in Europe, and I think the firm is committed to having an office in Europe,' Pran says. The affable Pran is already getting more work in Norway, and NBBJ is set to move southward. Though the particulars can't be revealed yet, Tom Morton, Joey Myers and Pran are designing a highrise in Frankfurt.

Not every story is a happy one. Pran was thrilled to win the international architecture competition and

National Gallery in Berlin

Interior of Deloitte & Touche Headquarters, New York

The interior for the advertising agency Deloitte & Touche is one of a number of sizable projects Pran undertook while at Ellerbe Beckett in New York.

Pran's first job in the US was for Mies van der Rohe in Chicago, where he worked on the National Gallery in Berlin (1963–68).

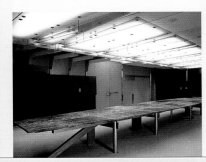

Seoul Dome, Korea

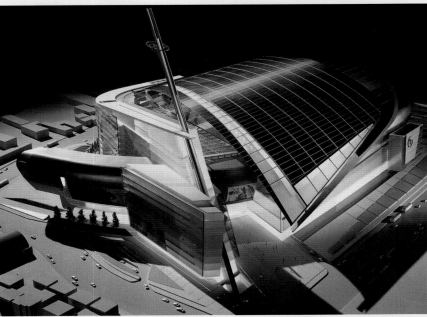

In 1997, NBBJ won an international competition to design the Seoul Dome, to host the 2002 World Cup. It was designed by Dan Meis and Pran, design principles, together with lead senior designers Jonathan Ward and Joey Myers and a large design team in the NBBJ Los Angeles office.

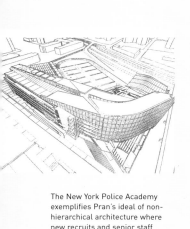

The New York Police Academy exemplifies Pran's ideal of non-hierarchical architecture where new recruits and senior staff are encouraged to intermingle.

to design the New York Police Academy in the Bronx in New York City, and to hear him tell it was well received by everyone. 'This is a non-hierarchical building, the brass and the recruits were meant to intermingle, and the idea was to open it up to the community.' The only person against using any budget money on any new building for the police was Mayor Giuliani. 'The NYPD, the Bronx community and the press strongly supported the construction and design of this building', says Pran.

Undaunted, the architect will continue to explore his ideas of free interchange and unrestricted movement. Fluidity and endlessness are 'liberating, in opposition to the more static aspects of modern architecture. I think it's an enrichment of modern architecture. It breaks down barriers, it opens up new horizons and it is also part of the informality of today's life. I would say 98 per cent of my buildings are asymmetrical, because I feel that most conditions in life or in the city are asymmetrical conditions. There's also an informality – it is not pompous or aristocratic architecture but a democratic and welcoming one.'

These ideals are shared with Pran's early influences and the fellow architects he respects the most. He values the work and friendship of Daniel Libeskind and Fumihiko Maki. They have influenced my spirit and thinking, not the specific forms in my work; I think they are two of the greatest architects and individuals today.

Pran would also like to follow the lead of Oscar Niemeyer. 'For him to be 92 and still be doing buildings, that's the way I'd like to be; when I meet him at his studio in Rio, he is always at work. I admire that. I do think I've had an exceptional life in architecture, a very rich life. And I would like to work in architecture as long as I live.' ⌂

New York Psychiatric Institute

State University of New York

Vintage Pran, the New York Psychiatric Institute and State University of New York are asymmetrical with ample glazing and connections to the community.

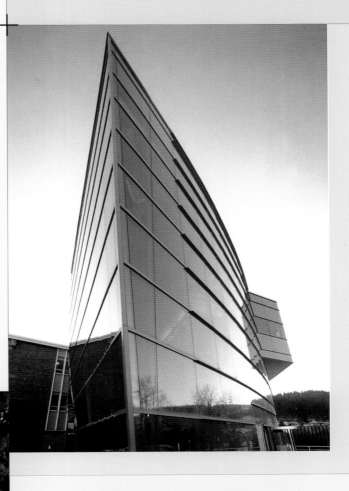

Kwun Tong Town Centre, Hong Kong

With projects in Asia and Europe, Pran is moving NBBJ towards a more global mindset. The Kwun Tong Town Centre by NBBJ was designed by Jonathan Ward, Joey Myers, Peter Pran, Dorman Anderson and Jim Jonassen.

Jakob MacFarlane

Robert Such

90s Sci-Fi
meets 70s High-Tech

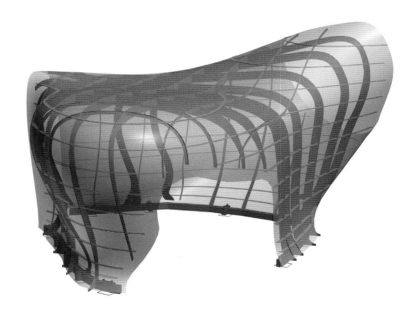

With the opening of the Centre Pompidou's 5th floor restaurant on 1 January 2000, Robert Such took the opportunity to find out how the architects were realising their amorphous forms for the High-Tech space – a process that necessitated a 'true marriag of mechanical desktop and Autocad'.

Before we tackle the story behind Jakob and MacFarlane's installation-cum-architecture at the Centre Pompidou, Paris, let us suggest a few possible similes. References to water suspended in zero gravity, the latest fruit pastel from Rowntree, larvae from planet Z or worms from a *Dune* film set all spring to mind.

So, with that out of the way, how do the architects see their work? 'How is more important than what' is Dominique Jakob's response, the objects themselves being less important than the concepts and process. Yet both are undeniably and inextricably linked and the outcome will be a sensual experience.

Four 5-metre high aluminium corpuscles, amorphous and hollow, house the cloakroom and toilets, kitchen, video room, and reception within the restaurant area on the Centre Pompidou's 5th floor of Piano and Rogers' monument to High-Tech.

Jakob and MacFarlane's entry, developed on Autocad, took them past the knock-out round of an international competition launched by the Pompidou Centre. Their strange globular entities were still only images on a computer screen, but in the next round they found themselves up against Philippe Starck and the duo François and Lewis. All of them had to submit a model and the software enabled the Franco-British team to produce 80 cm-thick slices in two directions, which were then assembled to take the virtual concept into the physical dimension and on to seduce the jury.

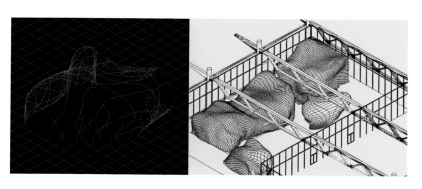

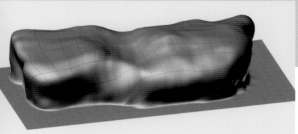

The competition brief called for a larger space that would cater for 300 visitors, while being able to hold a reception of a thousand. Otherwise, the constraints were minimal and provided generous room for interpretation.

Their adopted method is a non-linear pathway of creative exploration through a ping-pong of ideas across the table, combined with sketches and texts. Elements from one stage can become meshed into a later one, or an idea that failed to work in one step of the process can be used in another. According to MacFarlane it is a 'slow method, discovering how to work with the programme', but they 'started with a hands off approach [working with the existing context rather than starting afresh] and a position of minimising the impact of the object ... being there and not being there'.

Initial ideas for a series of mirrors that would reflect the exterior were discarded in favour of floating the restaurant by having a number of volumes hanging from the ceiling. These had the appearance of 'clouds passing through', but tended to mask Piano's blue, green and yellow plumbing.

Once brought down to the floor, hence creating buildings within a building, the emphasis remained on limited contact with the surrounding walls and floor. In contrast to the usual order of things, air conditioning, water, and electricity is piped down from above through holes in the structures.

The dictatorial modular frame of the Centre Pompidou exerted a strong motivation to work with the floor. They are scoring the volumes with the ubiquitous 80 cm by 80 cm grid, which is continuous with the borders of the aluminium floor tiles to give the effect of a deformed surface, although this almost failed to materialise as it was extremely difficult to find the software. They admit that they came close to dropping the whole idea of computer-generating the lines. With Mechanical Desktop, the American boat-building software, and Alain Duvivier at Alpha Link, however, their luck changed. Even though the pair acknowledge that if CATIA had been less costly it could well have made life simpler, the 'DIY' approach, the marriage of Mechanical Desktop and Autocad, has proved successful. MacFarlane gestures with his hands as he describes how they 'started with a void, followed by the suction up of the floor', which then enabled them to calculate the position of the lines on the 4 mm-thick skin and to locate any XYZ co-ordinates.

The aluminium itself, which will have a milled surface – rather than facetted as was first mooted – in order to create depth by catching and reflecting light, will be supported by a framework. A rubber lining, in either orange, green, red or yellow will differentiate one volume from another. Springs, on which the foundation beam rests, will pass through the lightweight, concrete, floating floor that replaces the former rusted metal panels.

Little internal support is needed, since the skeletons are light enough to stand alone, apart from the kitchen whose roof will increase to some 15 metres at its broadest point. This was requested by the Costes company, the second client to enter the arena, and indicates the flexibility of the architecture, in that it can remould itself to take in these volumetric alterations.

Folding planes, seen in their 1994 T House extension, playing down boundaries and juggling with private and public space, as found in the unrealised 1996 Puzzle House, can be traced from Jakob and MacFarlane's start up in practice in 1992 through to the present day. In addition, their concern with ambiguity offers different possible readings to Centre Pompidou visitors.

The latter has been explored further through partnership with Isometric – involved as lighting consultants – i Guzzini, and Halogen to create a virtual sun. During the day, the top-floor site benefits from the slow course of the real one, casting moving shadows over Jakob and MacFarlane's silvery landscape. As darkness descends, however, 320 dimmable QR 111 Halogen lamps take over. As one group of four bulbs dims, the next one will become brighter, thus imitating the imperceptibly slow track of an imaginary celestial object.

As well as specially designed lighting, Jakob and MacFarlane are working with Cappellini to make the furniture that is being shaped with the space in mind. The injection-moulded rubber chairs will be 'super simple' says MacFarlane and at the same height as the tables, thus having an even layer with an uneven surface rising above it.

A clear and striking presence is created by the unusual juxtaposition of these forms within Piano's High-Tech environment and Jakob and MacFarlane's work will surely draw positive and negative reactions in equal measure – just as the Centre Pompidou did in 1977. For a national art and culture centre that is no stranger to controversy, it will be par for the course. Go there and let your imagination run wild. ⌂

Central Artery/Tunnel, Boston

For two years, freelance photographer, Michael Hintlian has been recording the construction of the Central Artery/Tunnel, Boston, in the USA. The Central Artery is a six-lane elevated road, winding through the centre of Boston, built during the 1950s. Its current expansion to an 8 to 10-lane underground expressway, while the existing artery remains open to traffic, is one of the largest civil construction projects in the world. Hintlian has already received the ASMP Big Picture Awards 1999, Series Award, for his ongoing coverage of the work. Here we show a small selection of his photographs while he gives a brief personal account of the project.

Above top
River of Steel. Everett staging yard, August 1997.

Above middle
Tying rebar cage for new 'T' Station.
Lower State Street, Boston, August 1997.

Above bottom
Ventilator cage is guided by workers
as it is lowered into the slurry wall.
Near South Station, Boston, July 1997.

Left
Torquing rebar. Atlantic Avenue, Boston, May 1997.

Photographs by Michael Hintlian

When I first started to photograph and document the progress of the Central Artery Tunnel Project, I quickly realised that, beyond the magnificence of the engineering, it was the skill of individual tradesmen and women who would make this project a reality. I also realised that this would be the first thing that would be forgotten as we, the public, begin to use this tunnel when it is complete.

Over the past 28 months, I have documented the construction of the tunnel and the people making it happen. My interest is entirely in the human point of view, the meeting point of the work and worker, and what day-to-day life on this project looks like.

These photographs and my continuing work around this project seek to celebrate the workers, documenting what they do as the old artery is taken down and the new tunnel and bridge is built.

Michael Hintlian

Stephenson bell

At a time of globalisation when the standard seems to be set by high-impact architecture Stephensonbell – the architects of Manchester's new convention centre – are breaking the mould with some very sensitive and sensuous buildings. Maggie Toy investigates.

Often referred to as England's second city, Manchester has an industrial grandeur and grittiness second to none. Its prosperity in the19th century through cotton and textiles – due partly to the happy accident of its geography, close to shipping channels as well as the Lancashire and Cheshire hillsides that provided the right climate for milling wool and cotton – led to the construction of great buildings for a great commercial centre. Constructed from local sandstone, strong red brick, cast- and wrought-iron, they were conventionally topped in slate. The recent economic decline coupled with the erosion of wind and rain have since left the buildings dark and slightly weary. It's an architecture that can be intimidating, even bleak, but has an unavoidable emotional resonance. (At least for Macunians – I spent my childhood in one of the old mill towns that served the city.) Its scale, solidity and industrial aesthetic has also made it ripe for conversion into 90s building types, such as loft apartments, great barn-like bars and dockside shopping centres. It seems just as the decline of inner city Manchester was unavoidable in the Thatcher years, its current rejuvenation has been almost inevitable. The tragic desecration of the city centre by an IRA bomb let off in the Arndale Centre in 1996 necessitated rebuilding on a massive scale.

During the last decade or so, the work of Stephensonbell has become synonymous with Manchester: the two partners have been practising together in the city together since 1985, and previous to that were working together in an earlier incarnation of the firm. In 20 years they have produced 60 built designs for the centre. Roger Stephenson, the more senior of the partners, is the Macunian. Lively, he is perhaps even childlike in his energy and enthusiasm for both Manchester and the opportunities of building in it. In contrast Jeffrey Bell, with his dry Liverpudlian wit, seems to be the side of the partnership that provides the reality check, reeling Roger back from the edge of bouts of enthusiasm in order to extract the fantastic from the fantasy.

The practice's design work includes interventions within the streets of Manchester and responds to the existing context. The buildings do not shout out that they are designed by talented architects, the fact is only revealed when experiencing a building. Stephensonbell use local bricks to echo existing architecture, and their windows have deeper reveals to evoke the same robust appearance of those nearby. This is intertwined with details in metal and stone that ensure results, which invite comparisons with the way Carlo Scarpa chose to work in Venice – combining the beauty of the existing with the excitement of the modern.

Stephensonbell are aware of the existing financial challenges and attempt to be inventive to ensure their projects' economic success. A fine example of this is their own office, a 19th-century warehouse last used as a print works and more recently inhabited by junk, pigeons and dry rot. The firm had a minimal budget in which to renovate it (£23 per square foot). They worked closely with the client and produced a building that works within the existing structure. They tuned the use of materials and textures to express the space: the grand staircase that rises from the lower rooms to Stephensonbell's top-floor office changes material at each level and with it the feel and smell of the fabric.

Stephenson and Bell's identification with Manchester has led to a broader awareness of architecture's place in a city over time. They see their role as one of *bricolage* of cobbling or welding, rather than sweeping the slate clean and making a single mark. As they state, 'We see our task as one of weaving, patching and gap filling in the time-layered fabric of the city. Always clearly expressing the era in which we are working.'[1] It is as if they have made up their mind to be part of the perpetual motion of Manchester, referring to the past in how it has shaped the present, but also clearly expressing the time in which they are working. As they have written, since the late 1980s 'Manchester has been changing from a run down remnant of the prosperous Industrial Revolution City, to a vibrant new Metropolis. *It has been exciting to be part of this process.*'[2] ⟑

Notes
1. Stephensonbell, *Layers*, StephensonBell (Manchester), 1999.
2. Op. cit.

Situated next to the canal with excellent views over the historic waterside location and 4.5 m below road level this bar has become a focal point of the Manchester scene The use of strong, robust materials reflects the industrial heritage of the site, which, apart from being the location of a Roman fort was for a long time a sturdy depository for coal and slag. The scheme's aesthetic developed from the nearby road, the parallels of which reverberate into the site, expressed as layers of construction, and visibly dissolve architechnically across the site towards the waterside.

Due to be finished this year, this scheme provides Manchester with a much-needed central convention centre. The brief requires that the centre work as a stand-alone facility with a main, raked auditorium seating 800, an associated multi-purpose flat-floored hall, foyers and ancillary spaces. It also must work in conjunction with the neighbouring Gmex Exhibition Hall. Additionally, it must accommodate a building not yet constructed. On a site that is not level, this challenging brief has provided a platform for the architects' creativity and the results promise to be spectacular. (Built in collaboration with Shepperd Robson)

Quay Bar, Manchester

Manchester Convention Centre

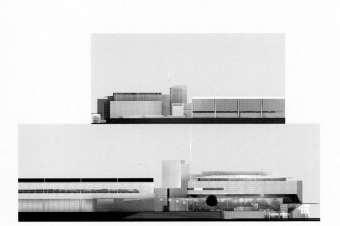

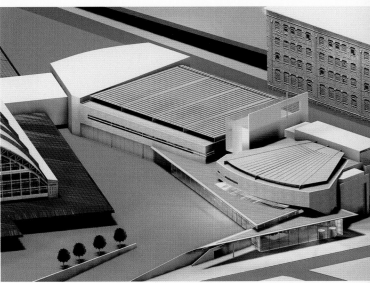

The basic plan form for this residential development utilised the existing stairways, conveniently sited to provide the vertical escape provision. The stairways are linked by internal streets on three levels within two lightwells. These function as gardens, providing an exquisite, restful oasis away from the bustle of the street as well as the means by which passive smoke extraction from the common spaces is achieved. This in turn enables a habitable room to be provided at the rear of each apartment, securing the maximum potential for this site with dual aspect homes. These have been particularly successful in encouraging a street community on the 'inside' of the building. Each apartment is split level with living accommodation on the real street side and sleeping areas on the quieter garden side. The detailing has yet to stand the test of time, but after two years it is still looking beautiful. The fact that there are queues of purchasers waiting for property in the building to become available is testament to the success of the scheme.

Stephenson bell

Smithfield Buildings, Manchester

Resumé

1969	Roger Stephenson qualifies from Liverpool University.
1971	Stephenson passes RIBA III and works with BDP, Manchester.
1979	Stephenson forms his own independent practice. In the same year, Jeffrey Bell joins him for his year out from Manchester Polytechnic.
1985	Stephensonbell is formed.
1987	Practice designs new conference centre at Manchester Airport.
1987–89	Remodelling for British Airways lounges and check-in facilities at UK Airports.
1992	Eastgate Development, Manchester. Conversion of warehouse to studio offices.
1994	UMIST development for offices and workshops.
1997	Practice wins competition to design Manchester convention centre.
1999	Warehouse conversion to apartments.
1987–99	Practice wins many local and national architectural awards and is featured in national architectural press.

Book Review

Jonathan Bell

Kenneth Powell *Architecture Reborn:*
The Conversion and Reconstruction of Old Buildings,
Laurence King Publishing (London), 1999, £45

As we rush headlong into the 21st century, the nebulous terms 'conservation' and 'heritage' play an increasingly important role in discussions about the built environment. Kenneth Powell, Consultant Director of the Twentieth Century Society, is well placed to observe the changing cultural perceptions of old buildings. His *Architecture Reborn* provides a comprehensive and authoritative overview of 44 restoration and refurbishment projects worldwide, each involving a significant change of use. The book, while placing an admirable stress on the difference between restoration and transformation, also reveals the disparity between the British and continental experience.

From William Morris' Society for the Protection of Ancient Buildings to English Heritage, the British conservation movement has a chequered reputation. The effect of wars on the built environment galvanised developers and politicians into recklessly disregarding the centuries-old patterns of towns and cities. Decades of destruction down the line, the tide finally turned. The rise of conservation movements and heritage bodies has coincided with increasing interest in previously dismissed building types – warehouses, mills, factories, industrial buildings, etc. The collapse of large-scale manufacturing industry turned the rebirth of the derelict and abandoned into pressing political concerns.

Re-use and transformation frequently confronts ideological and political associations as well as practical problems. Peter Lorenz's modernist extension to the At-Insprugg, a 15th-century hall heavily restored in the 1930s to serve as the HQ of the Austrian Nazi youth movement in Innsbruck, as well as Norman Foster's Reichstag, both confront the past, rather than bury it. Critics claim that by revealing the strata of occupation a building becomes a mere museum; for example, Foster's retention of mildly obscene Soviet graffiti in the Reichstag, dating from the building's wartime occupation. But leaving walls raw and unplastered is not merely kow-towing to unwarranted sentiment, it taps into the contemporary vogue for expressing authenticity and experience.

In examining the interface between old and new, Powell concludes that in the hands of an accomplished interventionist, historicism is, in practically all cases, unjustifiable. Tom Wolfe, in *From Bauhaus to Our House*, famously railed against Louis Kahn's Modernist addition to the Yale Art Gallery; contemporary thinking is not nearly as reactionary. *Architecture Reborn* presents an eclectic selection, leaping about in scale and location, from Richard Murphy's Edinburgh mews conversion to Me Di Um's Media Centre in Hamburg. The book is no gazetteer, but rather an overview and style sheet; a how-to manual that could act as a useful stick with which to beat heel-dragging conservationists and councils, and shock complacent corporations into re-thinking their new-build-equals-prestige mindset.

Making a clear distance from ham-fisted facadism, pastiche or reproduction, here is new architecture injected into old, often threatened structures. Britain is under-represented, almost certainly because of the vociferous and legislatively strong heritage lobby, which stridently oversees all interventions into our considerable historic fabric, with 1/2 million buildings on the official list. But perhaps things are changing, as political and social emphasis turns once more to cities, and the abundance of neglected and empty buildings. Interventions need not be overshadowed by the original, and it is clear that Powell advocates the approach that encourages innovation and exhibitionism. Renzo Piano's dramatic additions to Matté-Trucco's Fiat Factory in Lingotto would be unthinkable in Britain, where many industrial monuments have crumbled into dust, surrounded by yards of red tape and reams of legislature. One thinks of Architects' Co-Partnership's magnificent Brynmawr Rubber Factory in Wales, allowed to rot amidst political apathy, or the bruised and brooding hulk of Battersea Power Station.

Divided into four sections, 'Living and Working', 'Leisure and Learning', 'Museums Transformed' and 'Future Projects', this is an immensely readable and richly illustrated book, and one that makes good use of plans and sections to convey the alterations and additions. If there is a criticism, it is that it contains too few domestic projects . Given the shift towards the reuse of former industrial buildings as living space, analysis is lacking of how this phenomenon rapidly spiralled out of control, undermining the ethos of transforming redundant buildings through the creation of new-build 'loft-style' apartments. There are also no before and after photographs. Perhaps the picturesque charm of ruins threatened to be too distracting; a romanticist's vision of a fossilised, pre-Modernist world. You can transform all you like, but for many, the old, however derelict, will always be more seductive. ⌀

Minimalism has always struck me as uptight, no fun and full of guilty denial. No chance here for the deformed, the broken, the trace, or the-flawed-to-perfection. There is an urban myth, undoubtedly cultivated by the Minimalists, that to be a Minimalist one has to be especially good because of the attention to detail and the length of time one has to spend making things disappear. This trick of architectural disappearance could perhaps be called 'white magic'– a magic of reduction to phenomenological certainties. The play of the sun across a bare space, the erasure of blemishes in a no-fuss but lots-of-fuss sort of way, or the James Turrell-like virtual weight of a light object: these are the stock-in-trade tactics of the Minimalist. Taste can be a terrible thing when subscribed to by a dominant social class, the class from which most architects come. We seem to be suffering from a nasty rash of taste now, as the late 30-somethings and the early 40-somethings, graduates from the AA, RCA and the Bartlett in the early to mid 1980s, pepper our watering holes and restaurants with tasteful consideration.

So it was with some trepidation that I went with RCA graduate Jeffrey James to look around his recently completed foyer for brand consultancy Smith and Milton in Clerkenwell. James is immensely sociable, exceedingly well read, and for a man prone to the odd 'London night' (normally starting off at The Groucho), inquisitively lively.

The foyer, at first reading, is a well-executed essay in concrete and timber constructivist protocols. Such an approach is agreeable. The scheme consists of a series of walls, planes, tables and receptacles that create a landscape, things cut out,

things pushed in, things folded, light and shadow well considered. Photographs of the interior become Purist vignettes and remind one of some of Le Corbusier's daubings; there are resonances of Scarpa and Ronchamp but these are never literal. The interior as a whole is visually striking yet still maintains the air of corporate dependability and sturdy workman-like robustness. The functional detritus of office meeting, receptionist's pens, telephone and chilled *agua con gas* are all catered for and enjoyed as a creative opportunity rather than a designer's chore.

This is all well and good but there is another side to this seemingly tight and well mannered interior. If James is master of the white arts then he is also an apprentice of the black ones. As one becomes accustomed to the project's cool, pale face one becomes aware of another character of the work. Its beauty, like real beauty, is flawed; this calm interior landscape displays scars, scabrous crackings and gouged pockings. The floor even decomposes as it meets the boundaries of the space – disintegrating into large, flat, shiny, slate pebbles. Its more regular main surface is inscribed with an arch. What other geometries does James' work have up its sleeve? Or are these some sort of Cabalistic symbol? (I know that James has projected a contemporary Jewish Menorah for Hyde Park recently.)

Everyday objects seem to take on another quality within James' work. They appear strange or especially poised or just plain surreal. He has created a flower vase from a testube whose tumescence seems to have been boosted by testosterone. As one investigates further, one starts to see a few well-hidden brandings or castings or even hallmarks in the concrete. Smith and Milton are a branding consultancy. James plays on this idea of branding by making imprints of Smith and Milton's client's merchandise, the Jif lemon and Action Man particularly. The Action Man's head cast still retains some of the doll's hair. Fleetingly surreal images of a doll Pompeii float through my head.

For Jeffrey James has a love of craft, of the making of things – he lives above his own prototyping workshop. Not for him the tired steel-toe-capped boots and paint splattered overall however, but Nick Ashley coats and bright red sports cars. Salinger and Sartre are his companions on his aesthetic journey. ⚙